Hync

Edwardian Glasgow Tenement Suburb

Ann Laird

Published 1997 by Ann Laird
16 Dudley Drive, Glasgow G12 9SB

ISBN 0 9531571 0 5

Printed by Reproprint
10 Lynedoch Crescent, Glasgow G3 6EW

Inside Front Cover

Hyndland Farm in the 1890s

*This photograph was taken from 1 Princes Gardens, looking NW. The low, dark buildings of old
Hyndland Farm are at the far left, roughly where Crown Road North now meets Hyndland Road.
The whitewashed building stands in Prince Albert Road, Dowanhill. At the far right is Hyndland
Church, and to its right, the original Hyndland Station. Hyndland Road with its wooden fences and
street lights is clearly visible running right across the centre, with the fields of Hyndland Farm
continuing down over the slope beyond. Gartnavel Asylum sits on the distant hill to the left,
and the tall chimney in the middle belonged to Kelvinside electric power station.*

Photograph courtesy of Hyndland Parish Church

Contents

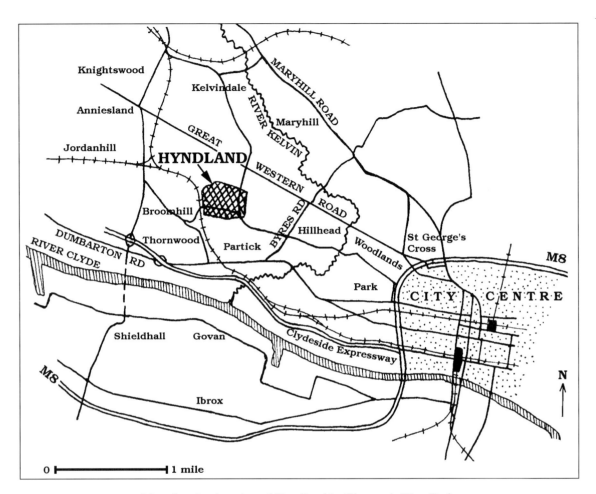

Map showing location of Hyndland in Glasgow's West End.

The development of Glasgow's West End gathered pace after the Botanic Gardens relocated to the Kelvinside Estate in the late 1830s, and Great Western Road was completed around 1839. Hillhead, Kelvinside, and Dowanhill estates were all largely developed by the 1870s, mostly with villas and terraces, which were built to very high standards designed to attract the wealthiest of Glasgow's population. By the 1880s, however, the need for housing a rapidly expanding middle and working class population had become pressing, and new construction turned more to tenements. Hyndland was one such development, in which a high density of housing was achieved, while retaining a degree of West End elegance and style befitting the people of the middle class for whom it was intended.

(A full account may be found in Glasgow West Conservation Trust's West End Conservation Manual)

Map courtesy of John Paton
History of the Development of Hyndland, Glasgow, and Evolution of its Urban Form, Unpublished MSc Dissertation, University of Strathclyde.

Foreword

Late in 1983, after the back courts had been upgraded, a chemistry teacher moved into her new Hyndland flat. The following spring, everyone waited for someone else to cut the grass, until, upon seeing an elderly neighbour on her knees using shears to clear a path to the washing line, the young teacher persuaded a dentist living downstairs to use his lawnmower. In a few years, she was organising the back courts for all 18 tenements in the block, and had seen every building inside and out.

Meanwhile, an explosion of information technology was taking place in the world at large and education in particular. The chemistry teacher had long since moved into computer education, and by summer 1995 had spent ten years in the thick of rapidly developing staff and pupil IT skills. The local history of her own tenement block presented itself as an attractive spare-time project in which local residents could participate, with the aim of producing a local history magazine on the computer.

Glasgow West Conservation Trust was called on for expert advice, work began in the Mitchell Library, and many local residents became involved. In June 1996, fifty of them attended a slide show and social evening. An exhibition, produced for the West End Festival, was later shown in the Mitchell Library.

About this time, "The Friends of Glasgow West" was set up, promoting conservation and amenity in the West End. Becoming a "Friend" provided many useful contacts, and led to collaboration on their first publication, "Listed Buildings in Glasgow West 1996".

When a close friend made a present of a rare old picture postcard view of Dudley Drive and Novar Drive, and the Trust simultaneously found one of Airlie Street, the hunt was on for any picture postcards of Hyndland. The Trust gave encouragement to extend the research, and after much labour in the Mitchell Library, the June 1997 exhibition was produced. When, thanks to Peckham's, it came home to Hyndland, the effect was magnetic!

Hyndland's local history was quick to encompass: the area is small and well-defined, the development is fairly monolithic and coherent, and the time is mostly confined to this century. Soon to emerge, however, were the close relationship of Hyndland not only to Glasgow but also to the nearby historic Burgh of Partick, and the important parts played by builders Duncanson and Henderson, and also by one of Glasgow's leading but perhaps unsung tenement architects, John C. McKellar, whose elegant designs characterise the heart of Hyndland.

This book follows the structure of the 1997 exhibition, and straightforwardly communicates the findings about Hyndland to date. However, the excitement of discovery, the never-ending supply of new questions raised as old ones are answered, and people's evident desire to know more about their past, will ensure that the real work on this local history is only just beginning!

Early History

The early history was researched by John Paton, in his "History of the Development of Hyndland, Glasgow, and Evolution of its Urban Form", unpublished MSc Dissertation, 1989, University of Strathclyde:

"The area known today as Hyndland was farmland until the late 19th century, and a farm steading with the name "Hind Land" was situated at the corner of the present Hyndland Road and Prince Albert Road. The name appears on maps and charters dating back to mediaeval times, and the land belonged to the Bishops of Glasgow, possibly being part of that granted to the Bishop by King David I in 1136.

"Following sale and dispersal of Church lands after the Reformation, "Hind Land" and the "Balgrie" lands adjoining to the north passed through various ownerships including that of William Anderson, a provost of Glasgow. Following Anderson's death in 1688 the estates were purchased by another provost, Walter Gibson, a shipping proprietor, merchant, and owner of nearby Partick, Whiteinch and Balshagrie estates.

"Hind Land, Balshagrie and Balgrie were sold on to another city merchant, Matthew Crawford, in 1720, passing to his son William in 1741 who died insolvent in 1755. In July 1759 Alexander Oswald, a merchant, added the estates to his existing ownership of Scotstoun and the lands remained in Oswald family ownership through several generations until the early 19th century when they were gradually divided and sold.

"Hind Land was bought by Rae Crawford of Milton in 1799, Balgrie by the owner of Kelvinside Estate, Dr Lithan – around the same time, and Balshagrie was retained by Miss Oswald of Scotstoun. Hyndland was now in separate ownership from the surrounding land and its boundaries remained unaltered until after development took place. The estate passed to Mrs Margaret Rae Crawford and then to her grandson, William Stuart Stirling Crawford in 1828". Crawford commissioned a feu plan in 1875, but then sold the estate in 1876.

The ancient Scottish "feu duty" system required land-owners to pay an annual duty to the "feudal superior" of the land. During the tenement era, most of Hyndland's feu duties were payable to the Trustees of the Church of Scotland.

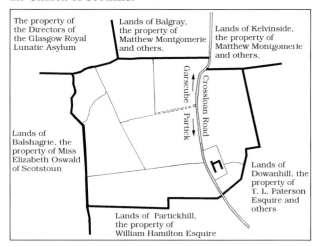

Ownership of Land Surrounding Hyndland Farm in 1870.

Feu Plans

In 1875, Hyndland lay outside the City of Glasgow, and there was no public transport: the nearest tram services ended at Kirklee and the railway line ran goods trains only. However, William Crawford, owner of the estate, commissioned City Architect, John Carrick, to prepare a feu plan. In his thesis, John Paton suggests that "terraces would have predominated, possibly set in gardens in the cases of those so named, in the style of Westbourne Gardens which had already been built in the adjoining estate" (Kelvinside). The next year, Crawford sold the estate to John Galbraith and Henry and William Bruce, but a severe depression in Glasgow's building industry reached crisis point in 1878 when the City of Glasgow Bank failed. Only two terraces were built.

By the mid 1890s, the horse-trams on Great Western Road came as far as Hyndland Road, passenger trains ran from Hyndland Station to the city centre, and Kelvinside Electric Power Station had opened at Hughenden (1893). Under these far more favourable conditions, the new owners of Hyndland estate commissioned surveyor James Barr to prepare a second feu plan in 1897. Their optimism was justified when the first of many feu contracts was signed the following year. Construction of the tenement suburb of Hyndland was at last under way! With only five of the twenty-eight tenement blocks remaining incomplete, and the "pleasure gardens", intended for the middle of each street, confined to Queensborough Gardens, Lauderdale Gardens, Dudley Drive and Airlie Street, the plan had been largely realised when building stopped in 1910.

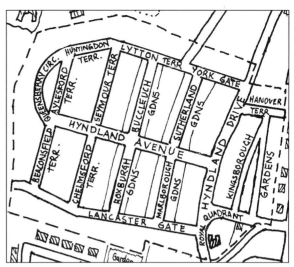

This unrealised scheme, which appears in Post Office Directory Maps between 1876 and 1883, was based on John Carrick's feu plan of 1875.

Map courtesy of John Paton

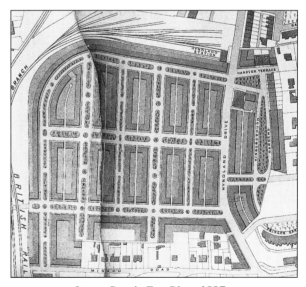

James Barr's Feu Plan, 1897

Map courtesy of Glasgow City Archives, Mitchell Library
Photograph reproduced by permission of Peter Reed

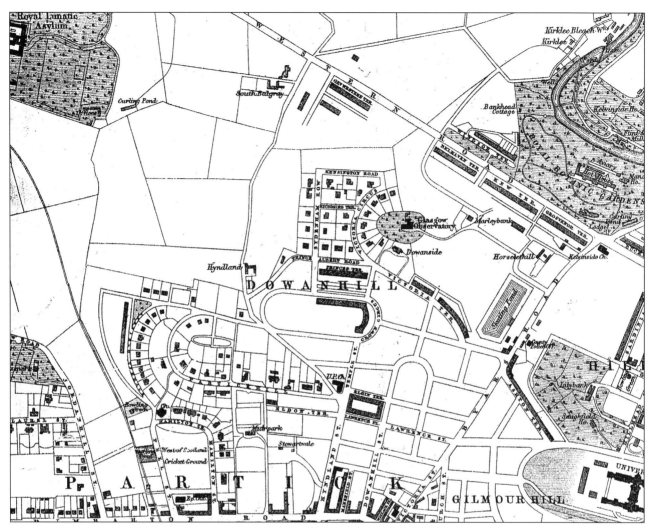

1870 Post Office Directory Map of Glasgow's West End.

The 'h'-shaped Hyndland Farm building can be found just to the west of Dowanhill. A curling pond beside the grounds of Gartnavel Asylum lies just beyond the north-west boundary of the farm land. Crossloan Road (not named on this map) runs northwards past Hyndland Farm, then along the side of South Balgray Farm and finally meets Great Western Road just west of Alexander 'Greek' Thomson's Great Western Terrace.
The villas of Dowanhill and Partickhill, each in its own generous plot of land, were all in place when this map was drawn in 1870, but the tenements of Hillhead, Partick and the Byres Road area of Dowanhill were yet to be built.

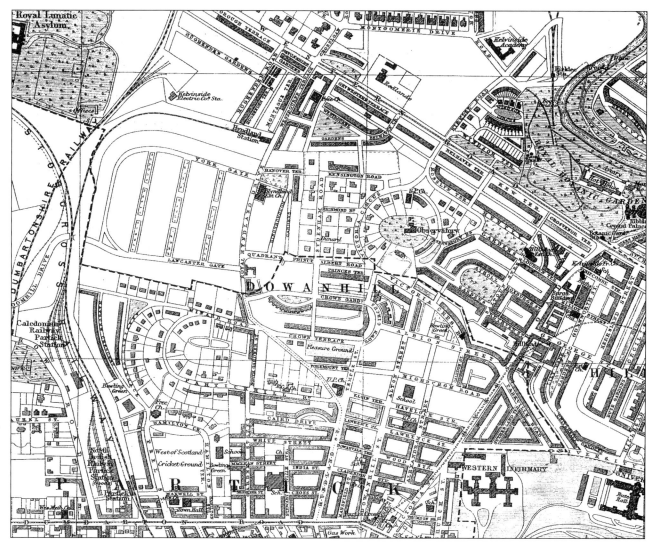

1899 Post Office Directory Map of Glasgow's West End.

In 1891, Kelvinside and Hyndland were added to the City of Glasgow and by 1899 many of the gaps in Hillhead, Partick and Byres Road had been filled in, very often with tenement building. Crossloan Road had been straightened, widened and levelled, and was now called Hyndland Drive. Hyndland Farm, however, remained completely undeveloped, apart from the north-east corner by the Railway Station. There followed 11 years of intensive building work, as almost the entire area of the old Hyndland Farm was covered with 4-storey red sandstone tenements.

Courtesy of Glasgow City Archives, Mitchell Library

AT POLWARTH AND AIRLIE GARDENS,
HYNDLAND NEW CAR TERMINUS.
3 and 2 R. and K. some with Maid's Room, Sculleries,
Electric Fittings, and Grates. Best Finished Houses in
Glasgow. Attendance 10 a.m. till 8.30 p.m., at 10
Queensborough Gardens, – Apply William MacKinnon,
34 West George Street.

AT QUEENSBOROUGH GARDENS,
NEW CAR TERMINUS, HYNDLAND,
OVERLOOKING BOWLING GREEN
4, 5 and 6 R. and K. with Maid's Room, Electric Fittings,
and Grates. Best Finished Flats in Glasgow.
Attendance, 10 Queensborough Gardens, 10 a.m. till
8.30 p.m.–William MacKinnon, 34 West George Street.

*Flats to let, built by the Western Property Company.
William McKinnon C.A. worked with Alfred Tongue &
Co., Chartered Accountants, who had another office at
86 King Street, Manchester.*

AT YORK DRIVE (Near Kelvinside and Hyndland Car
Stations). Best amenities in Glasgow. – Three
Beautifully-Finished, High-Class New 2 and 3 Room
and Kitchen Houses. Granite Columns at Entrances,
Large Parlours, Sculleries, Light Bathrooms, Electric
Light Fittings, Ranges with Tiled Surrounds, Polished
Mahogany Mirrored Mantlepieces with Art Tiled
Interiors; for Whitsunday, with early Entry. – Attendance
at buildings, 10 till 8, Mactaggart, 65 Bath St.

CLARENCE Drive, Queensborough Gdns, Hyndland,
near cars and Crow Rd Station – 4 rooms and kitchen;
electric light; light bath room; 2up; rent, £30; 3 rooms
and kitchen, from £25. – Mactaggart, 65 Bath Street
and 96 Queensborough Gdns.

Flats to let, built by J.A.Mactaggart and Co.

*These four advertisements appeared near the top of the
list of "Town and Suburban Houses" to let in the
Glasgow Herald of Monday, January 6th 1908. These
flats undoubtedly represented a most "superior class" of
tenement dwelling in Glasgow, with "light" bathrooms,
electric lighting, stained glass and many other luxurious
interior design features.*

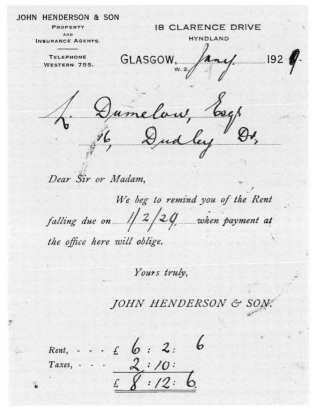

*Rent demand for a 2 room and kitchen flat (today called
a "one-bedroom flat") sent to a tenant at 16 Dudley
Drive by the "factor", John Henderson and Son, in
1929. Tenants in properties factored by John Henderson
and Son would have gone to pay their rent at the factor's
office at 18 Clarence Drive, one of a number of wooden
huts across the road from the main row of shops.*

*Hyndland's tenements had been built speculatively, in
common with most property in the West End, and over
the first few years there was considerable difficulty in
finding tenants, especially for the larger flats.*

The Tenement – a Way of Life by Frank Wordsall
(now out of print) is an essential guide to
understanding the history of Glasgow's tenements.

The Tenements of Hyndland

Hyndland was designed as an integrated whole, with great emphasis on symmetry, both in the overall layout of streets, and within each tenement block. At the residents' request, the developers added a bowling green into the original plans. Opening out Queensborough Gardens provided the required space, and, more importantly, gave the grid-iron layout a much-needed focal point. The steep slope adds a dramatic touch as the tenements tower over one another going up the hill.

Glasgow tenement architecture, which improved in many ways during the nineteenth century, reached its zenith in the early years of the twentieth century in developments such as Hyndland (1898-1910). Three factors combined to bring this period to a definite end: a trade recession which began around 1905; Lloyd George's People's Budget of 1909 which imposed new taxes, both on builders' profits and on the creation of new feu duties; and finally the outbreak of war in 1914.

The typical Hyndland tenement was a four-storey building of red sandstone, with a slate roof, canted bay windows, stained glass in the stair windows and front doors, tall chimneys, and modest front gardens with ornamental railings. Decorative features included distinctive corner roofs and corner windows. Access to the flats, usually eight to a close, was via a common entrance, decorated with tiles which in some cases went right up to the top floor. Corner buildings often had a different internal layout from those in mid-block. In some streets, particularly where there were larger properties, each tenement had one or sometimes two 'main door' flats with separate entrances to the street.

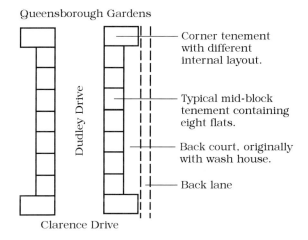

Layout of a typical street in Hyndland, with a block of tenements on each side

From the beginning, flats were generally let unfurnished. Property agents, known as "factors", collected a quarterly rent, and maintained whole buildings on behalf of the proprietors. From 1920 until the 1950s, rent increases were illegal, causing financial difficulty for proprietors and deterioration in the buildings in the long term. The Rent Acts of 1954 and 1956 allowed more realistic rents to be charged, conditional on repairs being carried out.

After the second war, owner-occupation began in earnest, and was the norm by the 1980s. This decade also saw the start of a new trend in short-term letting of furnished flats, typically to students and professionals.

Kingsborough Gardens, "B" Listed Building, Hyndland's first terrace. (Photographed in 1932)

This terrace, c1878-82, was Hyndland's first residential property, built by William Robertson. Standing to the west of all the existing properties in Dowanhill, it had an uninterrupted view over Hyndland Road, the fields of Hyndland farm and beyond, to Broomhill. Only Hyndland Church's little "tin church" stood nearby in Hyndland Road from 1878. The splendid isolation was soon ended when the adjacent Hanover Terrace was built around 1885, and the Railway Station opened in 1886. Meanwhile, William Leiper's Hyndland Church, one of the first red sandstone buildings in the West End, taking shape immediately in front of their windows, was completed in 1887.
The decorative cast iron balconies over the large entrances are not commonly seen in the West End.
In 1902, the property at the south end of the terrace was added, to a design by Woodburn Sturrock.

Courtesy of Glasgow City Archives, Mitchell Library

Hyndland's First Residential Properties

Hanover Terrace and Kingsborough Gardens

Hanover Terrace, "B" Listed Building, now part of Kingsborough Gardens. (Photographed in 1932)

Dating from about 1885, this was the second cream sandstone terrace built by William Robertson to appear in Hyndland. Both this and the Kingsborough Gardens Terrace were constructed on a rather larger scale than the later Edwardian red sandstone terraces, but they all conform to a similar general pattern. Because of the dangerous drop down to the basement, the cast iron railings on both of these older terraces escaped being sacrificed during the Second World War. Hyndland's first terraces relate far more closely to contemporary terraces in Dowanhill and Kelvinside, than to its own tenement development 15 years later.

Courtesy of Glasgow City Archives, Mitchell Library

The top of Clarence Drive, before 1910

The tenements of Clarence Drive were built early on, this being a main thoroughfare.
The tram lines (1910), the school building (1912), and the Clarence Drive shops (1926) all appeared later.
In the foreground are highly ornamental cast iron railings of the same floral design used on all the early tenements in Hyndland. Just beyond, on the slightly later buildings, the railings are plainer in style.

Although the Western Property Company employed architect J. C. McKellar almost exclusively, it was Alexander Adam who, in 1899, designed the tenements at the very top of Clarence Drive and round into Hyndland Road, easily identified by the ogee (bell-shaped) decorative roof on each corner.

Duncanson and Henderson
and the Western Property Company

Extracts from the recollections of the late Mr John Henderson (1886-1971),
the son of John Henderson, builder, of Duncanson and Henderson.

"Sometime prior to the year 1880, 'The City of Glasgow Bank' failed, and because it was not a 'limited company' the shareholders of the Bank were ruined when all their possessions were seized. There was a great gloom in the city and a vast amount of unemployment.

In 1898, Duncanson and Henderson, who had been clerks in a measurers' office (quantity surveyors) decided 'why not start in business for ourselves?', and thus the firm of Duncanson and Henderson came into being. Solicitors by this time were advising their clients to invest in property and as a result the clients felt secure with their investment.

Duncanson and Henderson immediately started to build tenements. They were not builders in the ordinary sense of the word. What they did was to prepare schedules from the architects' plans, and submit them to the various tradesmen to be priced.

Duncanson and Henderson purchased the ground bordered by Hyndland Road, Clarence Drive and Novar Drive down to where Dudley Drive enters Clarence Drive.

In 1898 the Western Property Company was formed, the shareholders being mainly Duncanson and Henderson. Building started in Hyndland immediately, and by 1910, in comparison with what already existed, very superior tenements of 3, 4, 5 or 6 rooms and kitchens had been built. Whole tenements were to sold to property companies. There was however little demand for the larger flats at that time, and these tenements remained more or less empty. In 1909 Alex Walker, the City Assessor, found that under some old Act, he could tax unlet property and proceeded to do so, creating an additional burden on the builders.

Fortunately, a great deal of difference was made to the letting of the properties when the tramways came to Highburgh Road in 1907 and were extended to Clarence Drive in 1910. This happened after Glasgow Corporation had been approached by Duncanson and Henderson with the idea of bringing tram services to Hyndland.

Between 1910 and 1919 many flats still lay empty. By 1917, a Limited Company was formed, and Duncanson and Henderson's affairs were handed over to Glasgow Heritable Trust Ltd. At a later date rents were controlled by Government action. Fortunately the same Act prevented Bond holders from demanding repayment.

From the 1920s until the early 1950s, the two companies, that is, Duncanson and Henderson and the

Western Property Company, now being run solely by Mr Henderson, owned flats in about 70 properties in Hyndland. Rents were controlled, and the Hendersons (John Henderson and Son, Property Agents) acted as factor for their own properties and also for many belonging to other proprietors.

After the War individual flats began to be sold, and the cash received from these sales began to accumulate. In 1951, the Inland Revenue proposed to tax the profit on the sales of flats. An appeal was lodged and was heard by the commissioners. The Inland Revenue was not satisfied by their decision and brought the matter before the Special Commissioners. The case was won when the argument that they were not a trading company was upheld – they did not buy and sell, they only sold!

In 1960, a public company, Glasgow Heritable Trust Ltd, was formed and absorbed the Western Property Company.

John Henderson and Son (Property Agents) continued in the factoring business until the late 1980s when the grandson of the original John Henderson retired."

Extracts courtesy of the Henderson Family.

(Left) Airlie Gardens to the South of Clarence Drive, viewed from Minard (now Turnberry) Road.

The postcard gives the location of these McKellar tenements as Partickhill, and indeed thirteen tenements altogether, in Airlie Street and Dudley Drive, fell within the boundary of the Burgh of Partick. The tall Partick gas-lamp on the street corner confirms this, when compared with the much shorter Glasgow gas-lamps everywhere else in Hyndland.

Postcard view of Airlie Gardens, courtesy of Bill Spalding

(Above) Airlie Street to the North of Clarence Drive in 1907

This scene is highly unusual in showing work in progress: a gang of workmen is laying the road and a line of Mactaggart tenements stands partially complete in Novar Drive. The tall chimney of Kelvinside Electric Power Station dominates the view to the north. All tenements in the foregound are by J C McKellar. To the right, long flights of steps leading up to the entrances, very tall chimneyheads, and the striking McKellar "Scots Baronial" corner roofs lend an imposing air to the upper side of the street.

Courtesy of Bill Scobbie, Hyndland Bowling Club

(Above) Dudley Drive, around 1910

Construction started simultaneously at two points in Hyndland, Dudley Drive, by J. C. McKellar, 1898-99, being one of them. The tenements here have relatively simple features. Notable, however, are the highly ornate Victorian railings contemporary with those on the west side of Hyndland Road and top of Clarence Drive. In Dudley Drive, only one example of these railings survives. During the 1941 Blitz, five tenements were destroyed in Dudley Drive. They were rebuilt to a different design in the early 1950s.

(Right) Queensborough Gardens, around 1908

Some of the finest examples of McKellar's work are in Queensborough Gardens, Falkland Street, and the corners of Polwarth Street and Lauderdale Gardens on the square around the bowling green. To the right, there is a large sign in a gap site where builder Robert A. McCowat, who was connected with Duncanson and Henderson, built tenements to a McKellar design in 1910. Open fields in the distance are a clear reminder that in Edwardian times, Hyndland was a suburb on the edge of the city.

The tenement at the far right (John Short, 1898) differs from all others in Hyndland, being of cream, not red, sandstone. This property was the first one proposed when tenement building commenced in Hyndland Road.

Postcard view of Queensborough Gardens courtesy of Glasgow West Conservation Trust

18

John Campbell McKellar, Architect

J. C. McKellar (1859 - 1941) was one of the foremost tenement architects in Glasgow, designing about 640 tenements between 1890 and 1910. He also operated his own vigorously entrepreneurial building company, John C. McKellar Ltd, which was very successful in building tenements in such places as Crossmyloof and Maryhill.

Wishing to improve the lot of the working classes, and believing in home ownership, he devised a highly innovative plan to encourage tenants to buy their own homes with a deposit and quarterly payments – unheard of in Scotland at the time. Unfortunately, deepening economic recession and the 1909 Finance Act struck at the roots of the tenement building culture, and McKellar's building stopped. After the First World War, he declined to participate in building the new local authority housing schemes, of which he strongly disapproved. He remained a prominent Conservative and member of the property-owning lobby in Scotland until his death in March 1941.

(from an article by Nicholas J. Morgan, *Dictionary of Scottish Business Biography*, 1986)

John C. McKellar

Courtesy of Glasgow City Archives, Mitchell Library

Alexander Adam, Architect

Early in his career, Adam worked briefly with John Short, producing, for example, designs for tenements at the east end of Partickhill Road. For Hyndland, in 1899, he designed just two adjacent blocks, in Hyndland Road. In 1901-2, Adam designed an ice factory and cold store in the city centre. He continued as an architect until 1939.

John Short, Architect

John Short produced plans for only one tenement block in Hyndland, for builder William Murgatroyd. He started his working life as a clerk of works to various builders, then began building on his own account, and finally reached the status of an architect, designing 210 tenements in only seven years from 1892 to 1899.

Falkland Mansions, before 1910

In Falkland Street every tenement has a main door flat. The plans for the block on the right are dated 1900 and those for the block on the left, 2 years later. The gap site, not to be built on until 1910, is clearly visible beyond the tenement block at the left. The 'aedicule' decorating the first floor bay windows to the left is typical of McKellar's most stylish properties. The same feature may be found on the McKellar tenements in Camphill Avenue, Langside. Falkland Street scores highly in having conserved a large proportion of its original windows.

Polwarth Street, around 1910

All the tenements in this postcard view are J.C. McKellar's. The end of Polwarth Street is blocked off by Novar Drive, and to the right, the tenements turn the corner into Queensborough Gardens. Seen from this angle, Hyndland Bowling Club resembles a charming country cottage.

Courtesy of Bill Scobbie, Hyndland Bowling Club

Clarence Drive at Dudley Drive, August 1953

J.C. McKellar's tenements stretch to the foot of the hill on the left. Across Clarence Drive, the north part of Dudley Drive, which is just visible at the right, was designed by Andrew Mickel. There was a tram-stop on each side of Clarence Drive at Dudley Drive, and local residents of the 1950s found the service frequent and reliable. For years Clarence Drive suffered from severe flooding under the railway bridge whenever the Hayburn Culvert overflowed after heavy rainfall. Remedial works were eventually carried out in the 1980s.

Photograph by R. B. Parr / STTS Collection, courtesy of David Brown

Novar Drive and Dudley Drive, around 1913

The tenements of Novar Drive (formerly York Drive) stand on each side of this view. Architect John Nisbet designed these properties in 1903-05 for builder John Mactaggart. The end of Novar Drive is marked by Queensborough Gardens running at right angles, and is lit by the streaming sun. Some of the central trees are clearly visible.

The next block is part of Dudley Drive, nos 33-46. Architect Andrew Mickel designed these properties in 1901-02, and again John Mactaggart was the builder. The sunlit sloping awning on the corner of Clarence Drive belongs to the St George Co-operative Society (later known as the Drive Supermarket).

The original postcard of which this is an enlargement was posted in November 1915, during the First World War, to an address in Paris. The card had been published locally by F. R. Chisholm, newsagent, whose shop was next to the station in Hyndland Road.

J. A. Mactaggart and Company

"Although the Scottish construction industry produced a number of men of enterprise and vision few can match the achievements of Sir John Mactaggart (1867-1956). His building work was of immense importance to the development of Glasgow and the West of Scotland between 1890 and 1940, and hc also made major contributions to housing policy in Scotland, the United Kingdom more generally, and the United States. In addition he was a generous benefactor to his native city, gifting parkland in 1930, and giving generously to the Empire Exhibition of 1938. He was a promoter of the Scottish Film industry, and on a wider stage promoted international understanding through the American and British Commonwealth Association, which he founded in 1941." (Nicholas J. Morgan, *Dictionary of Scottish Business Biography*, 1986)

Between 1901 and 1910, Mactaggart's building firm, J. A. Mactaggart and Co., developed the north-west corner of Hyndland, forming part of his total production of 300 tenements in Glasgow. The flats typically had a modest number of rooms but a high standard of internal amenity, matching the demand for middle-class housing. He employed Andrew Mickel to design the north part of Dudley Drive (1901-02). Novar Drive (1903-07) and the north part of Airlie Street (1907-10) were by Nisbet and McNair. The Western Heritable Investment Company Ltd and Mactaggart & Mickel Ltd came to the fore later, with extensive suburban developments after the First War.

Andrew Mickel, Architect

Following in his uncle Robert Mickel's footsteps, Andrew Mickel (1878-1962) managed a huge variety of building projects in Glasgow from the 1890s onwards. One of these was for J. A. Mactaggart, preparing plans for Dudley Drive north of Clarence Drive in 1901-02. In 1919, Mickel joined in business with Mactaggart, and they proceeded to revolutionise housing in the Central Belt.

John Nisbet, Architect

Having been an assistant to Frank Burnet and Boston, John Nisbet (1868-1951) set up on his own account in 1901. He worked extensively with J. A. Mactaggart, creating tenement developments in his own distinctive style, Camphill Gate, Queen's Park, being one of his finest. He also produced Mactaggart's own home, Kelmscott, in Pollokshields. Nisbet left architecture in 1910, when he handed over the practice to his assistant, C. J. McNair, and instead became the Inland Revenue's District Valuer for Dunbartonshire and District.

Charles James McNair, Architect

C. J. NcNair (1881-1955) was born in Ayr and apprenticed in 1898 to James A. Morris. Having joined John Nisbet in 1903 as a junior draughtsman, in 1910 he succeeded to the practice. With partner Robert Elder, the practice produced many of the "super" cinemas of the 1930s (Most of their Art Deco designs of this period were the work of the retiring and gifted Robert Elder).

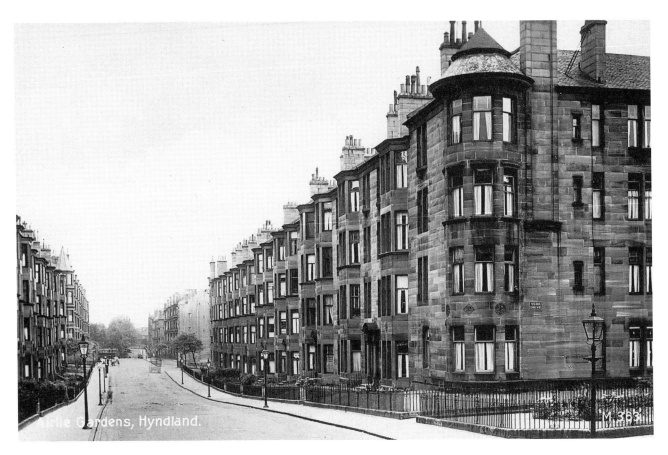

Airlie Gardens, Hyndland.

Airlie Gardens from Novar Drive

These properties designed by architects Nisbet and McNair have pink granite columns at the close entrances, shields carved in the stonework over the ground floor bay windows, and smoothly curved window ledges at top floor level. Their distinctive exterior decoration is unique to this part of Airlie Street and nearby in Novar Drive, although more of this type may be found in Broomhill. To the right, there is an unusual corner roof.

Novar Drive was formerly known as York Drive. The old street name is still clearly visible on the tenement wall.

The name "Airlie Gardens" has been carved on a plaque at the far end of this block, and probably refers to the buildings rather than the street. This name was commonly used by local residents, and also appears on postcards, but "Airlie Street" has always been the official name on maps.

Novar Drive (formerly York Drive)

This curved and exceptionally long row of tenements forms a "curtain wall" which hides the railway line behind, and encloses the north-west corner of Hyndland. The tenements in this view were designed by architect J. Nisbet in 1903-07 for builder J. A. Mactaggart. Six of them have Nisbet's distinctive pink granite columns decorating the entrances.

Hyndland was at one time a place where a great many families were brought up even in flats with just one bedroom, and in contrast with 1997, children were a common sight in the streets. This view is from the 1920s.

In Novar Drive above Lauderdale Gardens, there are two institutions for the children of the 1990s: Novar Nursery School and the 44th Glasgow Scout Group.

Kingsborough Gardens, early view.
These "pleasure gardens" are wide enough to allow comfortable use for leisure purposes.

Courtesy of Glasgow West Conservation Trust

George Spiers Kenneth, Architect

G. S. Kenneth was an architect with a large tenement and warehouse practice. For example, in 1899, he prepared plans for a Warehouse at 69-71 Queen Street, Glasgow, and some 3-storey & basement tenements, in Beaumont Gate, Glasgow, both "B" Listed Buildings. In 1901, G. S. Kenneth designed three tenements adjacent to the Parish Church in Hyndland Road, and in 1902, four red sandstone terraced houses in Kingsborough Gardens, all for builder William Benzie. The Kingsborough Gardens terrace houses are "B" Listed.

David Woodburn Sturrock, Architect

Little is known about D. Woodburn Sturrock, (c1860 - 1934) except that he was briefly partner with John Gordon and Son and David Bennet Dobson. From 1907 until 1918, partner with J. Jackson Wilson in Sturrock & Wilson.

D. Woodburn Sturrock did, however, design most of the red sandstone terraced houses in Kingsborough Gardens for William Benzie between 1899 and 1903, all "B" Listed.

William Benzie & Company

William Benzie & Co, Builders, developed the part of Hyndland to the east of Hyndland Road between 1899 and 1905. Construction of blocks of red sandstone terraced houses in Kingsborough Gardens alternated with groups of tenements on the east side of Hyndland Road, by architects D. Woodburn Sturrock and G. S. Kenneth. The tenement flats on the east side of Hyndland Road are well-appointed and of very generous proportions.

The red sandstone terraced houses of Kingsborough Gardens are almost unique in Hyndland amongst so many flatted dwellings. With their circular bay windows, dormers under circular roofs, entrances decorated with stained glass, and excellent condition, the houses have a particularly charming air. The original title deeds and the West End Local Plan prohibit subdivision, so all the properties have remained as full houses – a most unusual attainment in Glasgow.

*Tenement in Hyndland Road, designed by
G. S. Kenneth for W. Benzie in 1901.
This tenement's exterior shares many features with the
contemporary Kingsborough Gardens terrace.*

Kingsborough Gardens, south end, in the 1930s.

Courtesy of Glasgow City Archives, Mitchell Library.

Decorative Features of Tenements

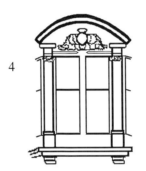

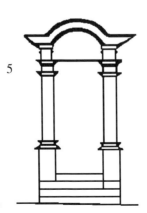

John C. McKellar, Architect

1 "Scots Baronial" multifaceted corner roof, Clarence Drive.
2 Decorative parapet and tall chimneys, Queensborough Gardens.
3 Low conical "Chinese hat" corner roof, Queensborough Gardens.
4 An aedicule at a first floor window, Falkland Street.

John Nisbet, Architect

5 An aedicule with granite columns at a close entrance, Novar Drive.

Alex. Adam and John Short, Architects

6 Ogee (bell-shaped) corner roof, Hyndland Road.

Explanatory note: an aedicule is an entrance or window which is framed with columns and crowned with a pediment.

Decorative Stonework

Part of the facade of a tenement in Falkland Street (McKellar, 1902)

In this building, as in all Hyndland tenements, the sandstone is cut as large squared "ashlar" blocks, with smooth polished faces. These blocks are built up in regular layers or "courses" with finely mortared joints. The stonework at ground floor level is "rusticated" ie it has strongly emphasised recessed joints, and the lowest few courses have roughly textured faces. Moulded "string courses" run horizontally across the facade, dividing each storey from the next.

Stair window, Lauderdale Gardens

Courtesy of Stephen Richard, Friends of Glasgow West

Decorative Glass

Between 1870 and 1914, Glasgow became an important centre for the production of decorative glass for the villas, terraces and tenements of superior quality in the West End. Hyndland's front windows, stair windows, front doors and interiors were no exception.

Sadly, in a hundred years, much of this fragile inheritance has been lost through ignorance, neglect or vandalism. Renewed awareness and interest in the decorative glass in Hyndland and the rest of the West End could help to conserve what remains.

Front door, main panel, Falkland Street

Courtesy of Stephen Richard, Friends of Glasgow West

Decorative Tiles

*A pair of "Glasgow Style" tiles
from a close in Polwarth Street*

Courtesy of Stephen Richard, Friends of Glasgow West

Decorative Ironwork

Cast iron balcony, around 1880

Hyndland's oldest terrace in Kingsborough Gardens has cast iron balconies over its doorways.

Cast iron panel railings, 1901-1905

The red sandstone terrace houses in Kingsborough Gardens had this design of railing throughout.

Typical Hyndland wrought iron railings, from around 1900 onwards

In this example from Clarence Drive, a single decorative panel adds interest at the top.

Cast iron railings, floral design, 1898-1900

This pattern was used in two places in Hyndland: at the top of the hill on the west side of Hyndland Road, and at the foot, in Dudley Drive and Clarence Drive.

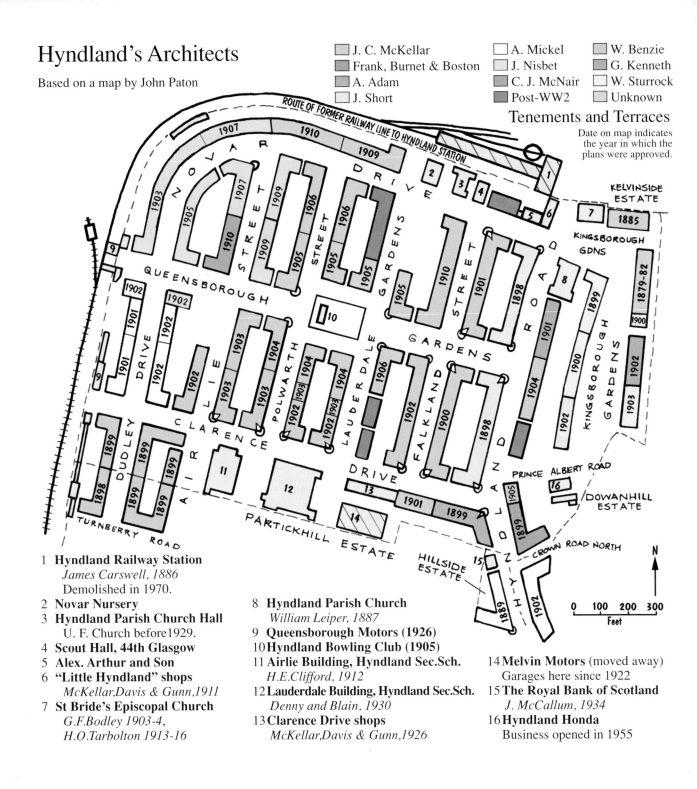

Hyndland's Architects

Based on a map by John Paton

Legend — Tenements and Terraces

- ☐ J. C. McKellar
- ☐ Frank, Burnet & Boston
- ☐ A. Adam
- ☐ J. Short
- ☐ A. Mickel
- ☐ J. Nisbet
- ☐ C. J. McNair
- ☐ Post-WW2
- ☐ W. Benzie
- ☐ G. Kenneth
- ☐ W. Sturrock
- ☐ Unknown

Date on map indicates the year in which the plans were approved.

1 **Hyndland Railway Station**
   James Carswell, 1886
   Demolished in 1970.
2 **Novar Nursery**
3 **Hyndland Parish Church Hall**
   U. F. Church before 1929.
4 **Scout Hall, 44th Glasgow**
5 **Alex. Arthur and Son**
6 **"Little Hyndland" shops**
   McKellar, Davis & Gunn, 1911
7 **St Bride's Episcopal Church**
   G.F.Bodley 1903-4,
   H.O.Tarbolton 1913-16

8 **Hyndland Parish Church**
   William Leiper, 1887
9 **Queensborough Motors (1926)**
10 **Hyndland Bowling Club (1905)**
11 **Airlie Building, Hyndland Sec.Sch.**
   H.E.Clifford, 1912
12 **Lauderdale Building, Hyndland Sec.Sch.**
   Denny and Blain, 1930
13 **Clarence Drive shops**
   McKellar, Davis & Gunn, 1926

14 **Melvin Motors** (moved away)
   Garages here since 1922
15 **The Royal Bank of Scotland**
   J. McCallum, 1934
16 **Hyndland Honda**
   Business opened in 1955

Hyndland's Early Residents

Kingsborough Gardens, Nos 2-16

from the Post Office Directory of 1892-93

Of particular local interest is J. Anthony Inglis, one of the owners of the large, successful Inglis' Pointhouse Shipyard in Partick. Many of the draughtsmen, engineers etc living in Dudley Drive would have worked there, or in the Henderson Meadowside Shipyard.

John McDougall, No 2, and **Daniel McDougall**, No 8, of "*McDougall and Sons*, wholesale and export glass and china merchants, glass engravers, china decorators and gilders, importers of foreign goods, 8-22 Jail Square."

James Anderson, No 4, of "*William Anderson and Co*, Manufacturers, 16 Princes Sq."

Matthew G Wilson, No 6, of "*John Wilson and Son*, Merchants, iron-tube manufacturers and brassfounders, Oxford and Buchanan Streets, Gorbals, and Govan Tube Works, Helen Street, Govan."

J. Anthony Inglis, No 10, of "*A & J Inglis, Engineers and Shipbuilders*, Whitehall Foundry, 64 Warroch Street; shipbuilding yard and slip dock, Pointhouse."

James Campbell Kemp, No 12 , of "*D. Kemp and Son*, silk mercers, shawl, mantle, costume and Scotch plaid manufacturers, 37 Buchanan Street."

James Macdonald M.A. LL.D., No 14 "*Rector, Kelvinside Academy.*"

James MacInnes, No 16, of "*William Graham and Co*, merchants, 55 Cathedral St."

Around Dudley Drive

2-6 Dudley Dr, 88-90 Minard Rd, 1-5 Airlie St
from the Partick Register of Electors, 1901-1912

Each occupation is counted once for each year it appears.

41	Clerk	2	Butcher
34	Engineer	2	Commission Agent
30	Traveller	2	Iron Merchant
24	Draughtsman	2	Jeweller
12	Book-keeper	2	Journalist
10	Joiner	2	Manufacturer
10	Teacher	2	Pawnbroker
9	Cashier	2	Sea-Captain
9	Manager	2	Steward
9	Photographer	2	Town Postman
8	Comm. Traveller	1	Baker
6	Accountant	1	Bank Messenger
5	Carpet Salesman	1	Bank Teller
5	Clergyman	1	Brass Finisher
5	Gentleman	1	Butler
5	Spirit Salesman	1	Chief Officer
5	Stockbroker	1	Confectioner
5	Tailor	1	Drapery Wareh'sman
5	Tobacconist	1	Drysalter
5	Warehouseman	1	Electrician
4	Blacksmith	1	Eng. Draughtsman
4	Cabinetmaker	1	Estate Factor
4	Grocer	1	Gas Collector
4	Organ Builder	1	Instrument Maker
3	Architect	1	Optician
3	Chemist	1	Physical Instructor
3	Dairyman	1	Retired Minister
3	Foreman	1	Saddler
3	Inspector, Public Works	1	Salesman
3	Litho Artist	1	Seaman
3	Minister/Journalist	1	Secretary
3	Painter	1	Ship Master
3	Plumber	1	Shipbuilder
3	Postman	1	Shoemaker
3	Retired	1	Stationer
3	Shipping Clerk	1	Student
3	Tea Merchant	1	Telegraphist
2	Boilermaker	1	Watchman

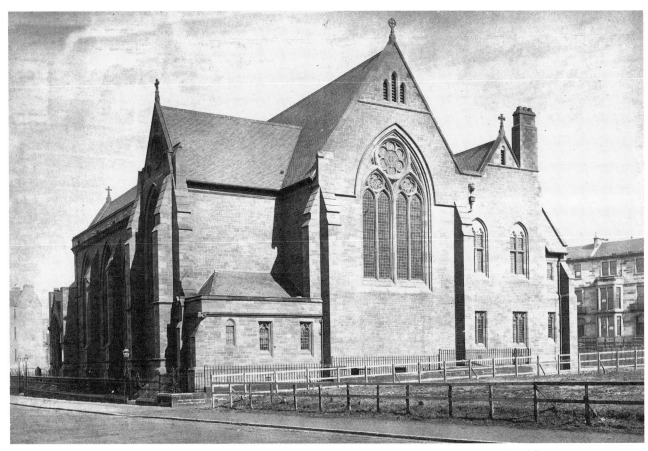

Hyndland Parish Church (William Leiper, 1887), Hyndland's only "A" Listed Building.

Behind the Church, to the right, is the first terrace to be built in Hyndland, in Kingsborough Gardens. Tenements built in Hyndland Road in 1901 now completely obscure this fine view of the Church.

Courtesy of Hyndland Parish Church

MINISTERS OF HYNDLAND PARISH CHURCH

John Service, D.D. 1878-1884
Henry John Graham 1884 -1906
Matthew Gardner, T.D., D.D. 1906-1939
John Lamb, C.V.O., D.D. 1923-1937

Edward T. Vernon, M.A. 1938-1947
James Hay Hamilton, M.A., B.D., J.P. 1948-1968
John A. Macnaughton, M.A., B.D. 1968-1989
John C. Christie, B.Sc., B.D. 1990-

Hyndland Parish Church

In common with many new churches of the day, Hyndland Parish Church started in a small way in a temporary building. In 1878, the "Tin Church" was moved from Byres Road to a position opposite the present Church on Hyndland Road. The congregation of Hillhead Parish Church could spare this temporary structure, having opened its own permanent church building on the corner of Observatory Road in 1876. Hyndland Church was thus created to serve Hillhead Parish Church's rapidly expanding congregation around the Hyndland Road/Great Western Road area of Kelvinside.

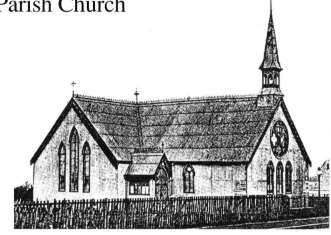

The 'Tin Church', erected in Hyndland Road in 1878.
Courtesy of Hyndland Parish Church

Hyndland Church was beautifully designed and carefully executed by William Leiper, in an almost mediaeval style, with no galleries. Dating from 1887, it was one of the earliest red sandstone buildings in the West End, the sandstone being transported by rail from the Ballochmyle Quarry near Mauchline in Ayrshire.

Although it was originally a chapel-of-ease of Govan Parish Church, Hyndland's largely Kelvinside congregation was easily able to afford to have its own Kirk Session and Parish. Having obtained permission from Govan Parish Kirk Session, Hyndland Parish Church became an independent entity in 1910.

It was not until after 1929, however, when parish boundaries were redrawn everywhere following reunion of the Church of Scotland with the United Free Church, that the tenement flats of Hyndland became the core of the parish.

In a recent major programme, first the exterior (1995), and then the interior (1997), were refurbished to the original high standard, the work being supervised by architect Iain Macrae of Frank Burnet, Bell and Partners. The total cost of around half a million pounds was in part supported by Historic Scotland, the balance being raised by members of the congregation and by the local community.

William Leiper, Architect

William Leiper (1839-1916), is famous for the former Templeton's Carpet Factory, Glasgow Green. His West End work includes Dowanhill Church, now the Cottier Theatre (1865), Partick Burgh Hall (1872) and Belmont and Hillhead Parish Church in Saltoun Street at Observatory Road (1875).

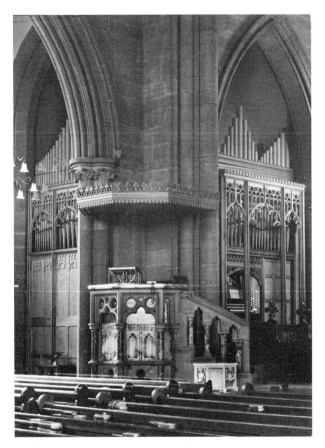

The three-manual organ by Henry Willis has been successively rebuilt during this century, making it one of the finest such instruments in the UK for performances of British turn-of-the-century music.

Present Church Organist:
John D. Langdon B.Mus., F.R.C.O.

The richly-sculptured pulpit is carved from alabaster and marble, and striking red and black tiles decorate the floor of the main aisle and altar.

Courtesy of Hyndland Parish Church

Oldest of the very distinguished collection of stained glass windows is a pair of small Guthrie windows depicting angels reading from Psalms. After the First War, Douglas Strachan was commissioned to design a memorial window for the gable end, featuring khaki-clad soldiers amongst biblical scenes. Other windows are by Douglas Hamilton, and after the Second World War, by Gordon Webster and William Wilson. The most modern window dates from 1969, and is by Sax Shaw. Following discussion with the congregation, a new stained glass "Community Window" in the north-east corner of the Church has been designed in contemporary style by a team led by Rab MacInnes, Hyndland Secondary School's Principal Teacher of Art. In 1997, funding was being sought for this project.

In 1929, a Church Hall was acquired at 24 Novar Drive in the shape of the former Hyndland United Free Church building. 1997 saw efforts being made towards expansion of local community uses of this Church Hall. In particular, Glasgow City Social Work Department was committed to run a pilot Lunch/ Community Information Club.

Russell House, situated in the tenement immediately adjacent to the Church, was dedicated in March 1997, in memory of Marian Russell MBE, and her husband Joseph. Russell House provides accommodation for the Church Officer and offers an opportunity for meetings.

Historical information from *Hyndland Hundred*, a detailed account of Hyndland and the first 100 years of its Parish Church, by Patricia Bascom and John R. Hume.

Hyndland Parish Church at the corner of Hyndland Road and Novar Drive, Summer 1996

Courtesy of Hyndland Parish Church

Hyndland Parish Church today serves the dense urban community of Hyndland, and is surrounded by tenements and terraces on three sides. The lack of Leiper's intended steeple is never noticed on this well-balanced church building. Close to the Church, on the corner of Novar Drive and Hyndland Road, is Hyndland's only block of cream sandstone tenements. Designed by John Short for builder William Murgatroyd, it is very similar indeed to another on the corner of Saltoun Street and Roxburgh Street, near Byres Road, which was the subject of the popular water-colour "Windows in the West" by Avril Paton in 1994.

Hyndland Railway Station (James Carswell, 1886), 66 Hyndland Road, in 1968.

Photograph courtesy of John R. Hume, Glasgow Stations

"This tall two-storey block had a projecting central section with a triangular pediment and symmetrical wings featuring a pronounced cornice and parapet. Clearly the architect wanted a variety of windows – triangular and curved pediments over the first floor windows, plain headers for the ground floor wings, and a large semi-circular fanlight to emphasise the entrance." W. A. C. Smith and Paul Anderson, *An Illustrated History of Glasgow's Railways*

In 1970, Hyndland's elegant station became its only major building to be lost to the demolition squads.

Hyndland Railway Station, Hyndland Road

In March 1886, the North British Railway Company opened a short branch from the Stobcross Line to the new Hyndland Railway Station (J. Carswell, 1886) on Hyndland Road. The rather grand design was in keeping with the fine terraces round the corner in Great Western Road. The platform was a lengthy one, with an iron and glass canopy at the station end to provide shelter for passengers.

In 1914, Hyndland was a busy station, with as many as 30 trains each way per day, mainly to and from Airdrie and Hamilton. A few years earlier, there had even been two through coaches from London, bearing "King's Cross to Glasgow (Hyndland)" boards and conveyed by the 11.20 am summer express!

By 1958, there were only 15 trains each way per day to the Hyndland terminus. The last passenger services ran in November 1960, and the imposing station building, which had the station-master's house in the upper storey, was demolished in 1970.

Major changes came about in the 1960s, with electrification and the advent of the "Blue Trains". Hyndland commuters soon recognised the vastly improved rail service at their new station on the main line, Hyndland being one of only two stations (the other being Partick) in the whole north-side suburban network through which all routes pass.

A large rolling-stock maintenance shed (Hyndland Electric Depot) was erected on the site of the carriage sidings, and a new through station to replace the old terminus was built only half a mile away. Eventually, even this Electric Depot closed in 1987 and the railway lines were lifted in 1988. Houses now occupy the site of the former railway terminus.

The site of the station became "Old Station Park". This was opened in 1985 on behalf of Hyndland Residents' Association by Mrs Winifride Logan, the wife of Hyndland's well-known local Councillor of the day.

A few yards to the left of this sign, a single short section of the old station's ornate Victorian railing remains in place beside the shops.

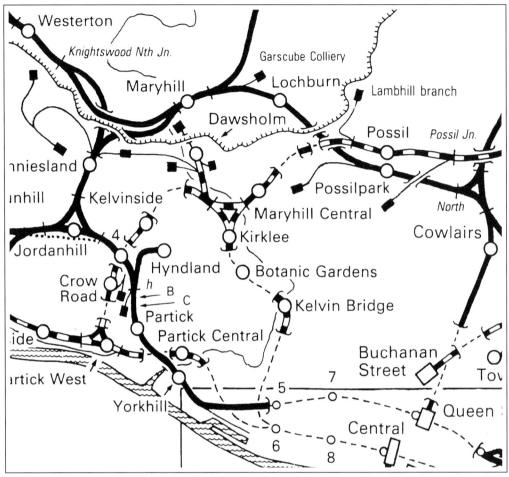

Map of Railway Lines in the West End

Courtesy of W. A. C. Smith, *An Illustrated History of Glasgow's Railways*

KEY TO MAP

h	Partick Junction
B	Partick Goods (Cal)
C	Partick Goods (NB)
4	Hyndland (from 1960)
5	Finnieston
6	Stobcross
7	Charing Cross
8	Anderston Cross

NORTH BRITISH

CALEDONIAN

The North British Railway Company's Stobcross Branch opened in 1874 and immediately became an important goods artery. This line ran southwards from Maryhill (where it linked with the existing Glasgow, Dumbarton and Helensburgh line), through Anniesland, Jordanhill, Partick, and Yorkhill to finish at the new Queen's Dock on the Clyde near Stobcross. In 1886, the line was continued as the Glasgow City and District Railway from Yorkhill via Charing Cross through to Queen Street Low Level, providing direct access to the City Centre from the West End, as it still does to this day. In 1886, the half-mile Hyndland spur was also opened, serving Kelvinside and Dowanhill. There were only three other buildings in Hyndland around this time: Hanover Terrace, the oldest terrace in Kingsborough Gardens, and the part-built Hyndland Church. Twelve years would pass before further development took place.

The Caledonian Glasgow Central Railway opened in the mid-1890's, linking Dalmarnock with Maryhill via Glasgow Central, Anderston Cross, Stobcross, Kelvin Bridge, Botanic Gardens and Kirklee. It was a remarkable railway, spending most of its passage through the city centre and western suburbs underground. From Kirklee the circle was completed back to Stobcross via Kelvinside station (beside the "Pond" Hotel), Crow Road station (below Clarence Drive at Westcars), Partick West and Partick Central. The most convenient station for residents in the lower part of Hyndland was the "Crow Road" station in Clarence Drive.

First to close was Botanic Gardens station in 1939, but Crow Road station operated until Hyndland electric station opened in 1960. British Rail finally ceased all services on the former Caledonian line in 1964.

Steam Train bound for Shettleston at the platform of Hyndland Railway Station in 1954. The square tower of St Bride's Episcopal Church rises behind the Station Building.

Courtesy of W. A. C. Smith, *An Illustrated History of Glasgow's Railways*

HYNDLAND STATION MASTERS
66 HYNDLAND ROAD

J. G. Brown, before 1896

W. P. Heron, c.1906-1916

George Good, 1916-1924

Thomas Durrant, 1924-1932

W. Porter, 1932-1936

P. Donaldson, 1936-1954

Pat McGlynn, 1954-1960

Pat McGlynn, the last Station-Master.

The McGlynn family moved into the station-master's house in the station building in 1954. He finally retired to Maxwell Park twelve years later, having been in charge of the new electric station for the last six years.

Photograph courtesy of Thelma Meechan

This sign, enclosed in a steel frame, was attached to the first lamppost in Novar Drive.

Photograph courtesy of Jim McGlynn

James Carswell, Engineer-in-Chief, North British Railway

James Carswell (c1833-97), who designed Hyndland Station in 1886 and Partick Station in 1887, became resident engineer of the North British Railway in 1869, and engineer-in-chief from 1879. His masterpiece was the roof of Queen Street Station. He engineered the Forth Railway Bridge approach lines, and was responsible for many buildings on the West Highland Railway, including workmen's houses at Fort William. In June 1884, on behalf of the North British railway, James Carswell acquired a curved strip of land from the proprietors of Hyndland Farm on which to bring the new short spur up to the terminus at Hyndland Road.

BBC Club

The former North British station gives Hyndland an interesting link with the BBC, between 1946 and 1962, when it was home to the BBC Club.

The BBC itself started in Glasgow in 1923 at Rex House, 202 Bath Street, transferring to offices in Blythswood Square in 1924. Its next move was to Queen Margaret Drive, where it opened on 18th November 1938. By 1946 there were enough staff to start a Club.

At first, the Club met in the Board Room in Broadcasting House, but the BBC very soon leased 66 Hyndland Road. The Club was officially opened here on 18th October 1947. Members had access to the Club six days a week, from midday until 11.30pm. There was a licence to sell drink from 7pm to 10pm. BBC staff of the day could relax with a whisky for 1/6d!

Table tennis, billiards, whist, drama and a library were all available for Club members. Badminton was played in a large studio back at Queen Margaret Drive, and the tennis section played at the Western Tennis Club for a number of years.

Hyndland Station in 1960.
From 1947 until 1962, the BBC Club used rooms on the ground floor.
Courtesy of W. A. C. Smith, *An Illustrated History of Glasgow's Railways*

The location of the Club at Hyndland Road, however, was never very convenient for Broadcasting House, and as early as 1951 members were asking the Committee to look for new premises. Eventually the BBC bought the building at 1 Botanic Crescent and the BBC Club moved there in 1962. It has remained in the same place to this day.

Historical information
from Ishbel G. Macdonald.

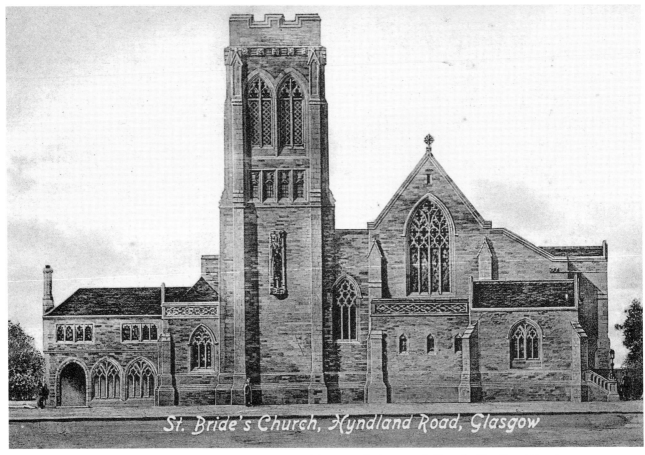

Postcard view showing drawing of St Bride's Scottish Episcopal Church, Hyndland Road.
St Bride's was designed by G. F. Bodley, 1903-4, with additions by H. O. Tarbolton, 1913-16.

RECTORS OF ST BRIDE'S EPISCOPAL CHURCH

Theodore Mansel Rhys Younghughes, 1894 - 1910	John Stewart, 1944 - 1953
Edward Thomas Scott Reid, 1910 - 1921	Ernest Tarrant Allen, 1953 - 1964
Oswald Paget Revely, 1921 - 1927	James Johnston Cleland, 1964 - 1973
Philip Charles Lempriere, 1927 - 1935	John Frederick Ames Farrant, 1973 - 1981
William Smith Robinson, 1935 - 1944	David McCubbin, 1981 - 1987

George Miller McMillan Thomson, 1987 - 1997

St Bride's Episcopal Church

The postcard view of St Bride's Scottish Episcopal Church shown opposite depicts the west front of the church as proposed by G. F. Bodley, the eminent Victorian ecclesiastical architect. He was commissioned in 1898 to prepare designs for a church in Hyndland to replace the wooden church situated at that time in Beaconsfield Road, Kelvinside, in which St Bride's congregation had worshipped since 1891. This small church, pictured overleaf, had been erected in the grounds of Douglas Castle in 1874 by the Earl of Home. When he had a permanent stone chapel built, he offered the wooden church to the Bishop of Glasgow and Galloway, who had launched an appeal for the building of more churches in the expanding suburbs of Glasgow.

However, Beaconsfield Road was not a convenient centre for the area to be served around Great Western Road from Kirklee Road to Anniesland Toll, with Kirklee and Kelvinside to the north, and Dowanhill, Partick and the developing Hyndland to the south. An endeavour was made to acquire a site for a permanent church at the end of Crown Terrace without success, but in 1899 a site was purchased at the corner of Hyndland Road and what was then Hanover Terrace. In what was described in a contemporary report as a "unique flitting", the wooden church was placed on wheels and towed by traction engines from Beaconsfield Road to Hyndland Road.

The chancel and the first bays of the nave were built and blessed in 1904. The remainder of the nave and north aisles were completed and dedicated in 1907 and

St Bride's Episcopal Church photographed in 1997.

*It is now designated a "B" Listed Building.
On the front of the crenellated tower is a niche with a statue of St Bridget.*

the first of the fine furnishings placed in the church. Bodley died in 1907 and it was hoped that the church would be completed within a few years. However, defective workmanship led to the abandoning of this work. It was several years before the church as it stands today was built to a modified scheme by H. O. Tarbolton, an Edinburgh-based church architect. He partially reconstructed the nave, added the double north aisle, and finally built the tower with the north-west entrance.

George Frederic Bodley, Architect

Bodley (1827-1907), a native of Hull and a pupil of Sir George Gilbert Scott, was one of Britain's finest Victorian Gothic architects.

By 1907, St Bride's had opened two mission churches: St Patrick's in Douglas Street, Partick, and St Faith's in Thornwood. Among the enormous number of workers and their families who had come to work in the shipyards and mills of Partick were many who claimed membership of the Churches of England and Ireland and who sought the ministrations of the Scottish Episcopal Church. These missions were opened to serve their needs.

There are five stained glass windows in the church, the two earliest by Edward Woore, one of which has the theme "Deliverance through Sacrifice" and is a thank-offering by a mother for the safe return of her three sons from the First War. The two windows on the north wall of the Lady Chapel are of exceptional quality: "The Nativity" by Karl Parsons and "The Sorrowful Mysteries" by Herbert Hendrie. A small window in the Chantry Chapel, by J. C. Bewsey, depicting St Mungo, the patron Saint and first Bishop of Glasgow, was

St Bride's Wooden Church at Beaconsfield Road, Kelvinside, where it stood from 1891-99.

J. B. Fleming, the owner of the Kelvinside Estate, in his 1894 book "Kelvinside", wrote about the "little wooden edifice recently erected in Beaconsfield Road" opposite his own house and sharing with it a beautiful situation and commanding a delightful view of the Clyde valley and the hills of the adjacent counties. The church was dedicated in honour of St Bride, the patron Saint of the Douglas Family, "The Earl of Home is the Son and Heir of Lady Lucy Elizabeth Douglas of Douglas, the last representative of the Noble Family of Douglas, and the Lands and Estate of Kelvinside are part of the Manor and Estates held by the Douglases, direct from the Crown".

Picture courtesy of Glasgow West Conservation Trust

installed by the congregation in 1920 to commemorate the appointment of the then Rector, the Reverend E. T. S. Reid, as Dean of the Diocese of Glasgow and Galloway. He was elected Bishop in 1921.

An illuminated scroll at the entrance to the Lady Chapel records the visit to St Bride's in May 1925, of Metropolitan Germanos, Archbishop of Thyatira, to celebrate the Liturgy of the Holy Orthodox for members of the Orthodox Communion residing in and around Glasgow. St Bride's has had links with the Eastern Orthodox Church since 1916 when twenty-two Serbian seminarians were exiled in Glasgow during the First War, and were placed under the spiritual care of the Rector of St Bride's. A Serbian Orthodox priest, Fr Dushan Markovitch, came frequently to celebrate the Liturgy and sing Vespers in St Bride's Crypt. At the present time a link has been forged with the Russian Orthodox Church by the visit of Fr Gennady Zverov, who became the first priest of the Russian church to visit Scotland since the demise of the Soviet Union. He attended a concert in St Bride's in aid of the Cameron Foundation, named after the eighteenth century Scottish architect who was commissioned by Catherine the Great to build palaces and the Cathedral of St Sofia, Pushkin. This Foundation is an "umbrella" for Scottish charities working in Russia, one of which has a connection with St Bride's and sends aid to the community around San Sofia, where Fr Gennady has organised the complete restoration work of the badly damaged Cathedral.

Historical information from David McCubbin.

St Bride's Church, Hyndland Road, Glasgow

This view dates from 1915. Since that date the interior has been further enhanced by additional fine carved woodwork. St Bride's possesses some examples of brass work by J. Wylie Davidson of the Glasgow School of Art, and a fine chalice and paten, the work of Jessie Newbery.

Perhaps St Bride's most interesting possession is a sculpture of the Blessed Virgin Mary and Child by Eric Gill dating from 1915. This is one of Gill's few works in Scotland.

Hyndland Post Office, 37-39 Clarence Drive, in 1937.

Courtesy of Glasgow City Archives, Mitchell Library

In 1901, a Post Office opened at 147 Hyndland Road. It was known as "Partickhill", for there was already a "Hyndland" Post Office, at the junction of Kirklee Road and Great Western Road. After some rationalisation in 1910, the sub-office in Hyndland was given its rightful name. In 1916, the corner main door flat at 1 Clarence Drive became the new home for the Post Office, and in 1919, Hyndland's new branch of the Commercial Bank of Scotland moved in to share this accommodation for its first two years. Once the Clarence Drive row of shops was built, the Post Office moved there around 1929.

John Murdoch was Postmaster from 1916, and in all, the Murdoch family gave almost fifty years of valued service to Hyndland. R. S. McColl took over the premises in Clarence Drive around 1965, and have remained there since.

Post Office

In 1910, according to the Post Office Directory, the Post Office did a marvellous job, with 6 deliveries daily, and collections from post offices such as Hyndland, 13 times a day. Telephones not being generally available, this rapid postal service was in great demand: a letter or card would normally be received on the day it was sent.

Postcards were a popular form of communication, with stationers selling local views. R. More, Stationer, Partickhill Post Office, sold the card below. It was posted on August 30th 1909, by a Miss M. Mudie of 16 Clarence Drive, to her sister in Wishaw.

Between 1904 and 1914, there was a great vogue for making postcard collections, based on themes such as churches or flowers, and mounted in albums.

Since the mid-1970s, these old postcards have become collectors' items, in demand whether depicting streets or buildings, tram or railway scenes, social life, or views of rural Scotland or further afield. A postcard view may offer the only illustration of a scene which has now vanished, and is therefore of real value to local historians. Postcard Fairs held at regular intervals give enthusiasts of all varieties the opportunity to indulge their magpie habits!

> Information about old postcards from Bill Spalding, member of Strathclyde Postcard Club, and author of local history books on Partick and Govan.

Reverse of the postcard captioned "The top of Clarence Drive, before 1910" (page 14).

The sender lived at 16 Clarence Drive, a little way down on the right hand side.

Hyndland Bowling Club soon after opening in 1905

Polwarth Street is to the right, and further tenement construction appears to be in progress in Queensborough Gardens, at the left of the Club-house. The Club-house was extended in 1932 by the addition of a wing at the left.

Hyndland Bowling Green was kept in first class condition by the green-keeper, William Stirling, from 1911 until his retirement in 1944. He was a most faithful servant to the club, and although he had to travel from Shawlands, was on the job every morning at 6am, and frequently worked late.

Courtesy of Bill Scobbie, Hyndland Bowling Club

Hyndland Bowling Club

Situated in the middle of Queensborough Gardens, the bowling green provides a welcome breathing space right in the heart of Hyndland. The 1897 street plans for Hyndland had originally consisted of unbroken rows of tenements, so the idea of including a bowling green in the middle provided a focal point for the area as well as giving the residents a recreation area, and affording the nearby flats a pleasant view.

Hyndland Bowling Club was founded in 1904 by Hugh M Mackie, Esq., C.A. He had recently moved into the district, and missing the bowling facilities of his native Stewarton, he saw the open space in Queensborough Gardens as an admirable site for a new bowling green. Quick action followed. Soon the proprietors of the ground, Messrs Duncanson and Henderson, were approached, and they gave their approval and support.

In the early autumn of 1904, meetings of the residents interested in the project were held, and the actual construction of the green and clubhouse was soon under way. The first full meeting of intending members was held in the new completed clubhouse on 15th December 1904, with Ex-Baillie James Mcfarlane presiding. The membership was 75 when the green was formally opened for play on 6th May 1905.

In 1931, because accommodation for all the teams playing on Match days had become impossibly cramped, the members approved an extension to the club-house, comprising a social room, kitchen and ladies' room. This work was completed the following year. To this day, the committee still find the facilities of the club most satisfactory.

In 1997, the Bowling Club is still very active, with its neat green and well-kept grounds and clubhouse. The sound of players enjoying their game is a familiar one in Queensborough Gardens during the long light evenings of summer.

The Founder of Hyndland Bowling Club, Hugh M. Mackie, C.A.

Courtesy of Hyndland Bowling Club

At the first Opening Day, on 6th May 1905, members and their wives attended the ceremony. Bowling clubs were very popular at the turn of the century, playing an important part in the social life of the community, and Hyndland was no exception. Messrs Duncanson and Henderson, the first Honorary Members of the Club, are sitting in the middle of the front row with their wives, and in the background is one of their very recently-constructed tenements at the corner of Polwarth Street. Mrs Duncanson threw the first bowls and was presented with a silver jack gifted by John and Robert Lawson. The first AGM was held on 7th February 1905, and the Club joined the Glasgow Bowling Association on 13th February. In that first season games were played with the Victoria Park, Willowbank and Partick Clubs.

During the First World War, the ladies' work party was formed and comforts of all kinds were sent to the fighting forces. Service men convalescing from wounds were received every other Saturday afternoon, and after a game on the green, were entertained to tea by the ladies, who in addition raised enough money to endow a bed in one of the military hospitals. In 1921, the Ladies' Club was formed. Wives, daughters and sisters of members were admitted as Lady Associates, with the privilege of playing on the green two afternoons per week. Their fund-raising work in connection with the green purchase (1928) and Club-house extension (1932) was invaluable.

Historical information adapted from
Hyndland Bowling Club 1905-1955
published by Hyndland Bowling Club

PRESIDENTS OF HYNDLAND BOWLING CLUB

1905-1955

1905	James Macfarlane
1906	James McCulloch
1907	Hugh M. Mackie
1908	John Lawson
1909	Alec Laidlaw
1910	H. Waller
1911	Isaac D. Scott
1912	T. W. Crawford
1913	R. H. Hopps
1914	W. Fraser Smith

Opening Day at Hyndland Bowling Club on May 6th 1905 Courtesy of Hyndland Bowling Club

1915	Dr. James Scott	1925	D. McKellar	1935	John B. Bodie	1945	D. MacDonald
1916	A. W. Meiklejohn	1926	J. K. Caldwell	1936	J. K. Caldwell	1946	H. C. Littlechild
1917	Andrew Gordon	1927	Duncan McPhail	1937	G. A. Stewart	1947	Andrew Paterson
1918	Andrew Little	1928	Dr. J M. Cockburn	1938	Peter Orr	1948	W. A. Harding
1919	C. C. Pengelly	1929	John B. Bodie	1939	L. M. Bennett	1949	M. M. Hair
1920	John Brodie	1930	A. S. Wright	1940	John G. Lunn	1950	Angus Kerr
1921	Alex. Smith	1931	E. D. Fairfoul	1941	William Traill	1951	A. D. Smith
1922	R. Robertson	1932	R. M. Smith	1942	F. L. Macpherson	1952	William Arnott
1923	H. J. Eastcott	1933	T. R. Inglis Melville	1943	Alex. Smith	1953	James Harter
1924	A. B. Allison	1934	J. A. Bulloch	1944	Dr. J. M. Cockburn	1954	Craig Kilgour
						1955	Dr. J. M. Cockburn

This postcard view shows a Standard Open-top Tram at the Hyndland Terminus between 1907 and 1910, prior to the extension of the route down Clarence Drive. The Post Office was at 147 Hyndland Road during this time, and the pillar-box can be seen on the left-hand pavement. In 1934, the house to the right of the tram was demolished and rebuilt as the new branch of the Commercial Bank of Scotland Ltd.

Postcard view of Hyndland Road, courtesy of George Lane, author of *Shooglies* and *Shooglies 2*

Tram Services

Hyndland's first electric tram service began on 4th December 1907, when the "Yellow" Langside – Kelvingrove service was extended to Hyndland via Church Street, Byres Road, and Highburgh Road. The Hyndland Terminus on Hyndland Road was situated between Crown Road North and Clarence Drive.

This "Yellow" route was extended to Broomhill Cross via Clarence Drive on 10th April 1910, partly in response to requests made to Glasgow Corporation by Duncanson and Henderson, tenement builders in Hyndland. It was thought that provision of a tramcar service in Clarence Drive might encourage more tenants to occupy the many empty flats.

In 1924, new track was opened linking Clarence Drive and Great Western Road. Two years later, the Clarkston to Kirklee "Yellow" service was extended on a loop which went via Highburgh Road and Hyndland Road, or via Byres Road and Great Western Road.

Previous tramway extensions had been laid with cobbled setts. However, the roadway in Hyndland Road was surfaced from the start in asphalt – possibly to placate local residents and the congregation of Hyndland Parish Church who had initially opposed this development!

Under a new numbering system introduced in May 1938, the old tram route identification "colours" began to disappear. Clarkston to Kirklee Circle became service number 5, and Langside to Anniesland, the 5A (24 from 1943).

After the Second World War, steady contraction of the tram services in the whole city took place at the same time as bus services began to take over. The last tram to run in Hyndland – in 1960 – was a No.10 (Kelvinside – London Road). However, dedicated tram lovers from Hyndland could still walk down to Dumbarton Road until 1st September 1962, when Glasgow's very last route (Dalmuir West – Auchenshuggle) went over to buses.

A No. 10 tram on the crossover in Hyndland Road, destination London Road via Bridgeton Cross.

The "clippie" is enjoying a breath of air on the upper deck.

Courtesy of David Brown, photographer unknown.

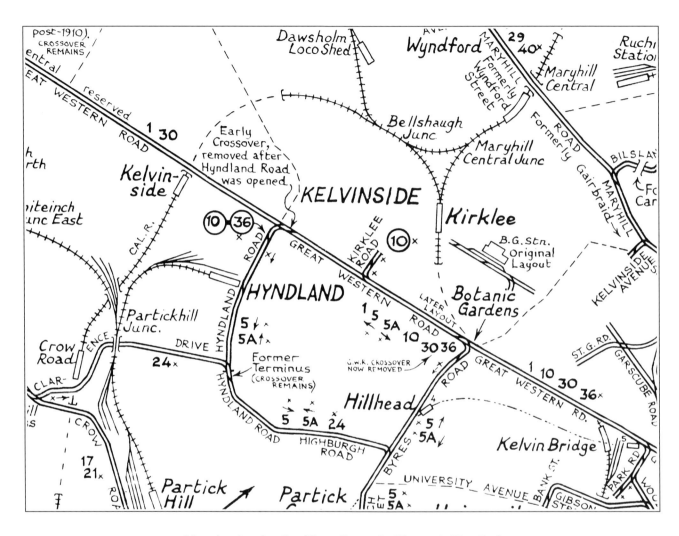

Map showing details of Tram Routes in Glasgow's West End.

Courtesy of John C. Gillham, Electric Railway Society

Postcard view of a Top-covered Standard Tram in Clarence Drive at Airlie Street,
shortly after the tram lines had been extended down Clarence Drive in 1910.

HYNDLAND'S BUS SERVICES

Bus Service No 5 began in 1929 (from Lennox Avenue to Muirend via Clarence Drive and Highburgh Rd).

Bus Service No 10 began in 1946.

Bus Service No 43 began in 1957 (replaced tram nos 5 and 5A).

Bus Service No 44 began in 1958 (replaced tram no 24).

Bus Service No 59 began in 1960 (replaced tram no 3).

Historical information from Brian Deans of the
Scottish Tramway and Transport Society,
PO Box 78, Glasgow G3 6ER.

The Airlie Building, Hyndland Secondary School, was designed by H. E. Clifford and opened in 1912. It is now a "B" Listed Building. Photographed in 1997.

Hyndland Secondary School

Partick Academy originated as a private school in Church Street, Partick, in 1850. In 1878, a new school building was opened in Peel Street by a group of gentlemen, mainly from Partickhill, who had formed the Partick Academy Co. Ltd. Very soon, major financial problems arose after the City of Glasgow Bank crash, and then in 1883 Govan Parish School Board announced its intention to build its own school nearby in Hamilton Crescent. Partick Academy succumbed to financial problems two years later, and the Board then leased their building until Hamilton Crescent School was ready in 1887.

By 1912, Hamilton Crescent School was overflowing, so pupils and staff moved into Govan Parish School Board's new "Hyndland High School" in Airlie Street, built at the edge of the nearby new tenement suburb of Hyndland.

Designed by city architect H. E. Clifford, it has many attractive exterior Art Nouveau features.

The Airlie Building originally had a central well and balconies with classrooms leading off, and accommodated 300 infants and 1100 older scholars! The classrooms were very well-equipped for the day with art rooms and chemistry and physics labs. Hyndland High School had a reputation for academic excellence, and many of its pupils went on to Glasgow University.

Hamilton Crescent School (Landless and Clifford, 1887), faces west across the Cricket Ground in Partick. Today it is known as Hyndland Primary School.

The Lauderdale Building, opened in August 1930 by the Lord Provost of the City of Glasgow.

Aerial view, Summer 1996, courtesy of Hyndland Secondary School

The Lauderdale Building was designed by Denny and Blain as an open "U" shape facing west. The fourth and lowest side of the quadrangle was added later. The open-air corridors, clearly visible in the photograph, were intended as a health measure against the spread of TB. Only one other school in Glasgow – Hillhead High School – still retains these open-air corridors today.

When the Lauderdale Building was opened in August 1930, 800 Secondary pupils moved in. Its highly innovative Domestic Science Department boasted a "house", furnished lavishly from floor to ceiling, which was a great attraction for visitors to the school. The Airlie Building continued to be used for 300 primary pupils.

During the Second War, the headmaster, Mr Andrew Hutchison, faced some difficult conditions. On 2nd September 1939, the main body of Hyndland pupils and teachers left Hyndland Station by train on a long journey to the safer areas, away from Glasgow. The Airlie Building was taken over by the military authorities at the outbreak of war, and in the following January the school re-opened officially with a reduced roll. The Primary Department met in the old Partick Academy in Peel Street and in Middlefield School in Partickhill Road. The school suffered the effects of blast in the Blitz of 1941, but came through the rest of the war with no further violent interruptions.

A notable feature at this time was the presence of refugees. As early as 1938, two Chinese girls had enrolled, having fled from the Japanese invasion. But during the war, refugees, many of them Jewish, came in greater numbers from Germany and Poland. The headmaster, Mr Hutchison, was first asked to take one boy, and as a result of the goodwill shown towards him, the Board of Guardians asked the school to take all the pupils requiring Secondary education, although their hostel accommodation, in Hill Street, was not in the catchment area. These young victims of Nazi persecution showed such ability and determination to succeed that nearly all obtained a pass in Higher English.

Post-War School Pupils 1946-47.

Photograph courtesy of Hyndland Secondary School

Teaching, administrative and janitorial Staff in the 1950s.

Photograph courtesy of Hyndland Secondary School

HEAD TEACHERS

Simon Fraser, F.E.I.S., 1900-19

John T. Dunn, F.E.I.S., 1919-29

Walter Jamieson, B.Sc.(Lond), 1929-38

Andrew Hutchison, M.A., B.Sc., 1938-45

David Carson, M.A., B.Sc., F.E.I.S., 1945-50

Samuel Weir, M.A., B.A., L.R.A.M., 1950-59

David B.C. Milne, M.A.(Hons), 1959-67

Francis Gillespie, M.A.(Hons), 1967-76

Donald A.M. Taylor, M.A.(Hons), 1976-85

Gerald G. Coyle, B. Sc. M I Biol, 1985-89

Kenneth Goodwin, M.A.(Hons), 1989-

Wonderful Trains

"Wonderful Trains" is a lively ceramic mural measuring 150 feet by 6 feet, which was designed and executed by pupils and art staff of Hyndland Secondary School. It was commissioned to celebrate Glasgow's year as "European City of Culture 1990", and decorates the entire length of the tunnel access to Hyndland Railway Station. This ambitious project was funded by British Rail Community Unit, West Area Management Committee, Glasgow District Council and Strathclyde Regional Council.

The early seventies saw major changes in Scottish Education, with the introduction of the Comprehensive system. Hyndland Senior Secondary and Hamilton Crescent Junior School were amalgamated to form the new Hyndland comprehensive. All Primary pupils were moved to the Hamilton Crescent building in Fortrose Street, and Technical Huts sprouted in the Hyndland playground to help accommodate the increased numbers of Secondary pupils.

A serious fire which started during the lunch break of Wednesday 12th October 1977 destroyed the Primary building in Airlie Street. The fire brigade found the fire fanned by high winds, and were hampered by low water pressure. They could not contain the blaze and much of the building was gutted.

After much uncertainty it was decided to undertake reconstruction. Work commenced in April 1979, with demolition of the remaining interior part and subsequent rebuilding with a new steel framed structure. During this time the pupils were accommodated in the Lauderdale Building and in the vacant Balshagray School. When pupils and staff re-occupied the Airlie Building they found dramatic changes: the central well was gone, replaced by a splendid lecture theatre occupying the ground and first floors, with new classrooms and new heating and ventilation throughout.

75 years after the opening of the Airlie Building, a large number of former pupils and staff joined with pupils and staff of the day in a major Jubilee celebration. There was an Exhibition and a Jubilee Magazine in which the history of the school was recorded. This Jubilee is fondly remembered by many former pupils.

Hyndland Secondary School today has Kenneth Goodwin as Head Teacher, and is, according to the HMI Report of March 1996, "a happy and a thriving school which has many strengths". Since the 1990s there has been a steady annual rise in school roll: in 1989 there were 500 pupils, and in 1997, over 880. There are many placing requests from outside the school's own catchment area.

Rab MacInnes, the school's Principal Teacher of Art, masterminded the "Wonderful Trains" ceramic mural for the Railway Station tunnel and has also designed a stained glass window which is proposed for Hyndland Parish Church. Hyndland is fortunate to have a school which makes such contributions to the community.

Shops in Hyndland Road

Only the further block of shops and tenements lies within the original boundary of Hyndland. In 1899, James Ferguson built several tenements on this corner of Crown Road North, to designs by Frank, Burnet and Boston.

The nearer shops and tenements to the right of this view were not built for another three years, and lay within the Dowanhill Estate, in the Burgh of Partick. They were designed by James M. Munro.

Postcard view of Hyndland Road, courtesy of George Lane, author of *Shooglies* and *Shooglies 2*

Shops and other Businesses

There are about 60 shops and many other businesses in Hyndland. These have been and still are one of its major assets, but their numbers are such that their history is a major study in itself.

Most shops in Hyndland were built in rows, either on the ground floor of tenement blocks, or as a single-storey block under one roof. A well-known corner shop was the St George Co-operative, at the foot of Clarence Drive, which opened around 1913, and served its customers for 60 years.

Other businesses and tradesmen, such as painters and decorators, slaters, boot repairers, property agents and garages, occupied wooden huts on empty sites.

Mrs Marshall's Sweetie Shop

People who were brought up in Hyndland remember Mrs Marshall's "sweetie shop" at the foot of Queensborough Gardens, near the entrance to the present station. Every morning the bread arrived from the baker on a horsedrawn cart, and mechanics from the nearby Queensborough Motors garage bought doughnuts there regularly. Children spent their Saturday pennies and halfpennies, buying such items as buttermilk dainties, soda lunches (in which a liquorice straw was used to suck sherbet out of a bag) and, if you could afford it, bottles of ginger for 2d, with a penny back on the bottle!

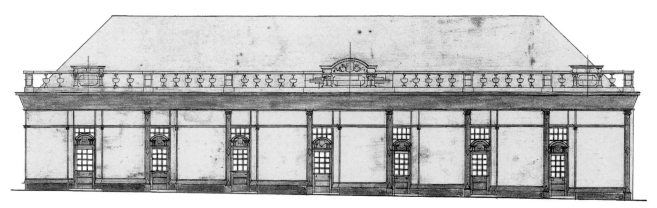

J. C. McKellar's 1911 design (front elevation) for the 'Little Hyndland' shops in Hyndland Road.

The Western Shops Company developed this site which had an excellent position beside the former Hyndland Railway Station, and also served Kelvinside and Dowanhill. Later, in 1925, the same company submitted plans for a row of 12 similar shops in Clarence Drive.

Courtesy of Glasgow City Archives, Mitchell Library

Hardie the Fishmonger on the corner of Clarence Drive and Lauderdale Gardens, around 1970.
This corner is now home to Peckham's Delicatessen .

Peckham's

"On 2nd August 1982, we first opened our doors at 43, Clarence Drive. The site which had previously been a fishmonger and then, for many years, a well-known toy shop, before a brief spell as an exclusive dress shop, was now a deli and grocers. The welcome from Hyndland was warm and encouraging if at times bemused – 'you're open 'til midnight but who would want to shop then?'. Wives told us that this was the one place that their husbands didn't mind shopping, and Peckham's girls and boys behind the counter left University and became today's doctors, lawyers, teachers and media producers.

In December 1984 the second door opened at 21, Clarence Drive – this time for a wide selection of fine wines, malts, liqueurs and of course the best Belgian chocolates. Fifteen years and several doors later, the Clarence Drive customers still seem to be the most involved, the first and most vocal with their thanks, praise, comments, requests or even criticism – many new products are tried out in Clarence Drive before being introduced to other branches.

We may have bigger and 'glitzier' branches elsewhere, but Clarence Drive is still regarded as 'home'. This highly regarded Scottish family company now employs some 200 people, but as it is written above the door at 41–43 Clarence Drive, this is where it all began."

Tony Johnston, Director, Peckham and Rye Ltd

Melvin Motors Ltd, Lauderdale Gardens

Melvin Motors Ltd was the last of a long line of garages in Lauderdale Gardens opposite the School, where now there is a red blaes playing field. Strictly speaking, this site lies partly in Partickhill.

During 1922–25, Hyndland Garage Ltd built workshops on this site, including a row of lockups facing into Clarence Lane (see 1926 photograph below), and an extension was added at the rear in 1936. The garage owner, William Slack, and his wife lived close by in a villa in Turnberry Road. On 13th March 1941, however, they met a sad and sudden end when their home was utterly destroyed by a landmine.

The garage, however, was left standing after the blast, and in 1956, Claud Hamilton (Motors) made major improvements which included a new showroom, petrol pumps with kiosk, offices, workshop and stores. An old air raid shelter still remained on the site.

Around 1965, Melvin Motors Ltd took over. A clerkess who worked there remembers it as a big, busy branch, with a thriving Radio Department where motorists had their cars fitted with the latest car radios.

In 1974, all Melvin's branches in the city closed down, and everything, including the Head Office in Kingston Street, moved to Minerva Street. Thus ended fifty years of car servicing on this site in Lauderdale Gardens.

Lauderdale Gardens from Turnberry Road around 1970.

Just across Clarence Drive, the two flat-roofed blocks of modern flats, one with six shops on the ground floor, had been built in the 1960s.

Courtesy of Glasgow West Conservation Trust

Garages in Lauderdale Gardens, in 1926.
The lockups on the left faced Clarence Lane behind the shops.

Courtesy of Glasgow City Archives, Mitchell Library

Aerial view of Hyndland Honda in 1990, just before extensive improvements were made.
The petrol pumps were removed and a new showroom was added.

Courtesy of Hyndland Honda

Queensborough Motors and Hyndland Honda

In 1926, the Henry family opened Queensborough Motors at the foot of Queensborough Gardens. In 1966, the adjacent Halley's site was taken over, including the showroom in Clarence Drive. Today the Mazda showroom is in the same commanding position. 1955 saw expansion to Prince Albert Road, with a filling station and some lockups. From 1961, the Albert Road site was gradually developed, and by 1986 had a new showroom, office accommodation and service centre.

In 1997, the Queensborough showroom at the foot of Clarence Drive displays the latest Japanese cars.

Broomhill Motor Company Ltd

The Broomhill Motor Company at the foot of Clarence Drive in 1926.
The Queensborough Mazda showroom was later built on the same spot.

After the War, Halley's took over from the Broomhill Motor Company. In 1966, when Halley's moved out of
the city to Milngavie, Queensborough Motors took over the complete site, stretching from Queensborough Gardens,
along the back of Dudley Drive to Clarence Drive.

Courtesy of Glasgow City Archives, Mitchell Library

Alexander Arthur & Sons Ltd, Building Contractors

Alexander Arthur & Sons Ltd was founded in 1948 by the late Alexander Arthur. It became a limited company in 1964, and moved from Paisley Road West to 4 Novar Drive in 1975. However, its Hyndland connections go back to 1946, when Alexander Arthur moved from Largs to live in Novar Drive, to be nearer his employment in the building trade. However, he soon started up in construction on his own account.

Over the years, the company has successfully completed a wide range of building and civil engineering contracts up to a current single value of 3.5 million pounds, including many major projects for the University of Glasgow such as the refurbishment of the Chemistry Department. Works in Hyndland include Back Court schemes at Falkland Street and at Dudley Drive, and alterations at Hyndland School.

The new branch of the Commercial Bank of Scotland at 162 Hyndland Road, late in 1934, with its stone and black granite frontage, and Egyptian inspired Deco ornament. The branch is now part of The Royal Bank of Scotland and has "B" Listed Building status.

James McCallum, the Bank's own Master of Works, drew up the plans.
Building materials were specified exactly:

Main Stonework – Cream Sandstone from Heworthburn   *Lower Courses – Polished Black Bon Accord (Aberdeen) Granite*
Windows – Steel Windows in Teak Frames   *Outside Doors – Teak*

Courtesy of Glasgow City Archives, Mitchell Library

The Royal Bank of Scotland

The Commercial Bank of Scotland opened its new Hyndland branch in December 1919, having appointed James T. King as manager. It shared premises with Hyndland Post Office, at 1 Clarence Drive.

The new branch was an immediate success, so much so, that in 1921, the branch moved to larger premises at 152A Hyndland Road in the corner flat across the road.

In 1934, with business continuing to grow, the Commercial Bank of Scotland purchased the residence at 162 Hyndland Road with a view to reconstructing the front portion of the building as a purpose-built bank. The splendid new branch was completed the same year. James T. King continued as manager until his retirement in 1946.

Bank amalgamations followed: in 1959, the Commercial Bank of Scotland merged with the National Bank of Scotland to form the National Commercial Bank of Scotland; this amalgamated again in 1969, and the Hyndland branch then bore the name "The Royal Bank of Scotland".

An automated teller machine was installed outside the building in 1982 to provide customers with 24-hour access to cash. During a major modernisation of customer facilities in 1997, the teak doors were replaced with glass, and the upgraded automated teller machine was relocated inside.

Former Residence at 162 Hyndland Road, early in 1934, just before it was demolished.

Courtesy of Glasgow City Archives, Mitchell Library

Historical information adapted from information provided by Archive Section, The Royal Bank of Scotland plc.

March 13th 1941 had been a pleasant, sunny spring day. Dusk fell on a quiet evening with a clear sky. The Tivoli Cinema in Crow Road was showing Charlie Chaplin in "The Great Dictator".

There had been very few air raids on Glasgow, most of the German bombs having landed on cities such as Liverpool, Coventry and London, so there was little indication of the terror to come. Yet that evening saw the start of a series of devastating bombing raids on the west of Scotland, forever printed on people's memories as "The Clydebank Blitz".

Many residents of Hyndland were to suffer that night. Mrs. MacPherson and her neighbour had enjoyed the film at the Tivoli – a first cinema outing for the young mother since the war began. The two women came out of the cinema, and hearing the distant explosions and seeing the glow in the sky over Bearsden, realised that an air raid was imminent.

At 9 Airlie Street, Hyndland, schoolboy Alan Sherry saw the barrage balloon rising from the nearby swing park. He too knew that an air raid warning would soon follow.

Mrs MacPherson and her neighbour returned to her flat further along Airlie Street, prepared for a long night ahead. Unlike most of the residents of Airlie Street and Dudley Drive, they refused to use the shelter in the back close, believing it to be a "death trap". Just before 11.30, the distinct sound of approaching Heinkel 111s was heard.

Members of the Home Guard, meeting at Hyndland School, rushed out at the news that a

Reconstruction of Heinkel 111 dropping landmine over Dudley Drive, on the moonlit night of 13th March 1941.

Landmine: Metal canister, (very like a large metal dustbin), 8 feet high, 2.5 feet across, packed with high explosive, drifts down on a parachute, detonated on contact or by a timer.

parachute had been sighted, prepared to arrest a German airman. However, that parachute carried something even more sinister – a landmine – more destructive than any bomb. Alan Sherry recalls hearing "a loud, sharp crack" which seemed to come from the sky. He later realised that this was the sound of the parachute opening, bearing the deadly landmine earthwards.

Landmine in Dudley Drive, 13th March 1941

This ceremony was on the spot where the landmine destroyed four tenements, and marked the handing over of a mobile canteen, a gift from the Canadian people to the people of Hyndland. The devastation in Dudley Drive is only too obvious. A huge gap is left where once there were tenements. Local children and adults are shown watching the proceedings. These tenements were rebuilt in the early 1950s.

There were three explosions in Hyndland, and others around the West End. One demolished a row of houses in Peel Street, opposite the West of Scotland Cricket Club, killing fifty people. Another blast destroyed a house at the corner of Lauderdale Gardens and Turnberry Road where two people were wiped out without trace. This blast blew in the windows of Mrs MacPherson's flat, along with the front door. The ceilings at the front of the flat collapsed.

The third devastating blast hit Dudley Drive, killing thirty six people and injuring twenty one, most of whom had been sheltering in the back closes. A mine had exploded on tenements between 8, 10, and 12 Dudley Drive, totally destroying them. Numbers 6 and 9 Dudley Drive were later demolished. Three people were trapped in 5, Airlie Street, immediately behind Dudley Drive. Mrs MacPherson recalls that in this third blast

Daily Record and Mail, *August 2nd 1941.*

Courtesy of the *Daily Record* and *Sunday Mail*

the back windows shattered and only the tight net curtaining which collected the glass as it shot across the room, saved her from serious injury. The remaining ceilings collapsed, leaving her covered in plaster and soot, dazed but not seriously injured.

Soon after, ARP (Air Raid Precautions) rescue teams and the Home Guard arrived, stretchering the injured to the shelter in the grounds of Hyndland School. As Alan Sherry and his parents made their way to the shelter, he looked up to see the Heinkel 111 silhouetted against the night sky above him. The flickering flames of a few incendiaries still littered the street.

The shelter had only basic facilities. The school janitor, Mr Langlands, and his wife raided their own meagre supplies, but there was little they could do. Casualties were brought in from Dudley Drive, some quite seriously injured, but there was a long wait for an ambulance, as most had been deployed to Clydebank. A.R.P. rescue men, led by warden Ian Buchanan, began to dig for survivors in the rubble.

The long night wore on and eventually an uneasy quiet fell. At 6.30 a.m., the Salvation Army arrived with hot water and tea. Alan Sherry recalls his father going off to work straight from the shelter, with only a shilling in his pocket. (He says that of course there was no stress counselling then. It was simply a matter of "getting on with it!") Mrs. MacPherson wheeled her baby's salvaged cot down Peel Street to her mother's later that day.

The grim task of digging through the rubble continued for many days, many residents being critical of the authorities for their "incompetence and lack of urgency". Alan Sherry, along with many others, recalls the story of a schoolboy called Stanley Ewing who was reportedly dug out of the debris after two and a half days. He claimed to have survived due to the fact that, shortly before the blast, his mother had sent him to the front room cupboard for some cube sugar. Entombed by the falling masonry, he stayed alive by eating the sugar and drinking the water from the fire hoses which dripped down through the wreckage!

Five hundred people had been made homeless by the blast. St. Peter's Girls' and Infants' School in Partick became a temporary shelter and later Hillhead High School housed survivors until they were able to find something more permanent.

Alan Sherry moved back into 11 Airlie Street and it remained his family home until 1960. Mrs MacPherson found accommodation in Kelvindale and was one of the first to return home, three months later, after repairs had been completed. She remembers the end of the war as "a time of thankfulness rather than joy", although her husband did hang a large flag out on V.E. Day!

The Clydebank Blitz took a terrible toll. Between 13th and 15th March 1941, approximately twelve hundred people were killed in the raids and over a thousand seriously injured. Many thousands were made homeless. The Great Dictator had left his mark.

Compiled by Janette Stewart
from reminiscences of local residents.

Delayed-action Bomb in Tenement

A bomb which had fallen inside a tenement in Polwarth Street finally went off around lunchtime on the day after the Blitz. No-one was injured, as the building had been evacuated. After rebuilding, this tenement was indistinguishable from the rest of the block. It is interesting to note that in Hyndland there were no cases of whole blocks of tenements being destroyed in the war.

Prisoner-of-War Camp

In the later part of the war, a party of 40 to 50 American soldiers was based in a small camp on the corner of Clarence Drive and Lauderdale Gardens. Wire mesh fences enclosed the area, and six to eight Nissen huts stood inside. The Americans held prisoners, including Italians, who required fairly low security conditions. Local residents report seeing the prisoners being taken on regular working parties by means of army transport, and also being exercised by walking up and down Clarence Drive. Children of the day regularly went up to the gates, where some of the troops would be hanging about on the other side, talking with American accents. Some of the soldiers were billeted in flats, and one resident recalls seeing their cunning method of getting coal upstairs – they used a small crane to lift the sacks and passed them in through the windows!

Public Air Raid Shelters

Air raid shelters recalled by war-time residents: one in the school, one in Novar Dive at Airlie Street, one behind the garage on the corner of Turnberry Road and Lauderdale Gardens, and an underground shelter near the lockups at the north end of Lauderdale Gardens.

Army Vehicle Repair Depot

The British Army commandeered part of Queensborough Motors as a repair depot for trucks and light tanks.

The Home Guard, photographed in the school.
Courtesy of Mrs MacPherson

Original Features Lost or at Risk in Hyndland

Traditional timber sash and case windows – *replaced by inappropriate modern windows*
Garden railings – *removed by order in the Second World War*
Stonework – *spoiled in some early stonecleaning attempts*
Tall chimneys – *lowered on safety grounds*
Roofs – *slates replaced with artificial tiles, appearance spoiled by untidy TV aerials and satellite dishes*
Front doors with decorative glass and original door furniture – *replaced for security reasons or personal preference*
Decorative tiles – *damaged by conduits/pipes for gas, electricity, stairlighting, door entry systems, cable television*
Swan-neck light fittings in closes – *replaced to meet safety requirements*
Decorative glass in stair windows – *lost or damaged through neglect*

Planning Permission

"Hyndland is a charming part of the city and as Councillor I am gratified by the respect and care taken by most residents in the area.

The planning system plays an important role in maintaining the unique environment of Hyndland. If you wish to make changes to your property there are specific steps to be taken and you should contact:

The Department of Planning and Development,
231 George Street, Glasgow G1 1RX.

It is possible to make some changes without planning consent, eg some interior alterations, provided the changes are not to a Listed Building.

Where planning permission is necessary it is generally the case that four copies of drawings are submitted together with the fee when you lodge your application. The Planning Department can provide information on notifying your neighbours of your plans.

In a Conservation Area or in the case of Listed Buildings more stringent controls apply. Information and forms are available from the Planning Department. Where Listed Buildings are involved, the case may be referred to Historic Scotland. Glasgow West Conservation Trust can also offer advice on a variety of conservation issues.

All the positive effort we put into maintaining Hyndland today will ensure future residents enjoy living here as much as we do."

Glasgow City Councillor Ruth Simpson, Hyndland Ward 13.

Glasgow West Conservation Trust

30 Cranworth Street, Glasgow G12 8AG
0141 339 0092

The Glasgow West Conservation Trust was established in 1990 as a registered charity with a remit to conserve the city's historic West End through investment, education, training and the promotion of high standards of repair and restoration.

In partnership with the City of Glasgow Council, Historic Scotland and the Glasgow Development Agency, the Trust encourages conservation research, sponsors lecture programmes, publishes technical information and co-ordinates capital grants for a broad range of projects.

The Friends of Glasgow West

c/o GWCT, 30 Cranworth Street, Glasgow G12 8AG

The Friends of Glasgow West is the support group for Glasgow West Conservation Trust and has interests in the amenity and conservation of the West End.

Kelvinside Community Council

Local issues in Hyndland may be taken to the Local Councillor or to Kelvinside Community Council, which holds monthly public meetings in Hyndland.

Conservation Area and Local Issues in 1997

In 1970, Hyndland lost one of its finest buildings, the Railway Station in Hyndland Road. Luckily, few other historic buildings in the area have been needlessly demolished. Over the years, however, many original features of Hyndland's handsome tenements have been placed at risk, whether from inadequate maintenance, prolonged neglect, safety regulations, deliberate vandalism, or simple ignorance of their intrinsic value. Hyndland is certainly not alone in this predicament – such problems extend across the West End and citywide.

During the 1960s, a Glasgow Corporation block of flats for the elderly in Hyndland Road, and a small private development in Lauderdale Gardens, were built with little regard to matching the surrounding tenements, as was common at the time. The private development of flats at the top of Novar Drive in 1980 shows a better attempt to blend in. More recently, the Lauderdale Mansions development of 1997 successfully incorporated a number of important Hyndland features, albeit in reconstituted stone, and in response to pressure from local residents. Rising population density also raises some concerns.

In an atmosphere of increasing national awareness of conservation, Hyndland's two churches were afforded status and protection as "Listed Buildings" in 1970. Glasgow Corporation designated the "West End Conservation Area" in 1972 and "Hyndland Conservation Area" in 1975. Planning authorities are obliged to "protect and enhance the character and appearance" of such areas. Around this time, Kelvinside Community Council and Hyndland Residents Association also worked to enhance the area. The Royal Bank of Scotland, the terraces of Kingsborough Gardens and Hyndland School's Airlie Building were all listed in 1987. Hyndland was finally amalgamated into the revised Glasgow West Conservation Area in 1990.

In 1986 the West End Local Plan was published by Glasgow District Council as part of a citywide exercise, meeting statutory requirements. Its policies and detailed objectives include Housing, Leisure and Recreation, Traffic and Transport, Shopping and Environment. The Planning Department can supply copies. After the reorganisation of local authorities, an updated Local Plan is expected from the new Glasgow City Council.

Planning controls in a Conservation Area are more strict than elsewhere. It is sometimes forgotten that trees are also protected and pruning methods recommended. The City Council can provide further advice.

Local issues in Hyndland in 1997 include:
- *Parking*: pressure from residents' and visitors' cars; obstruction of emergency vehicle access.
- *Grass-cutting in central "pleasure gardens"*: suspended during 1997 owing to City Council budget cuts.
- *Alterations carried out without Planning Consent.*
- *Absentee landlords and multiple occupancy.*
- *Proprietors'/residents' responsibilities*: stair cleaning and back court maintenance; organising common repairs to roofs, chimneys, walls, gutters etc.

Acknowledgements

Everyone's willing and generous response to my requests for providing access to local information, or for giving their time and expertise, has made research over the last two years into Hyndland's history a most rewarding and pleasant task. My warmest thanks go to all the following:

– *Glasgow West Conservation Trust's Gordon Urquhart*, whose manifest enthusiasm for and dedication to Glasgow's West End took a practical form in providing consistent support and extensive professional expertise throughout this project, including key advice on many aspects of this book. The Trust's West End Lectures and Conservation Masterclasses, and the West End Conservation Manual provided a unique "education".
– *Maureen Waddell, M.B.E.* for passing on her long experience of conservation issues in the West End.
– *Bill Spalding*, historical details and invaluable advice.
– *Mitchell Library staff*, especially in the City Archives.
– *Michael Dale*, for initiating the West End Festival.
– *John Paton*, for his excellent MSc thesis on Hyndland.
– *Many Friends of Glasgow West*, including *Philip Drew*; the *Stained Glass Survey Group*, Hyndland; *Alan Stewart*, architect, extensive local knowledge; *Donald MacAskill* (The Scottish Tenement).
– *John Cairney*, (John Smith & Son, Booksellers).
– *John Cowie* and *Liam Taylor,* (Sime Malloch), production of exhibition panels.
– *Iain Paterson*, for information on Glasgow's architects.
– *Lynne Carson Rickards*, for proof reading.
– *Tony Johnston* (Peckham's) for exhibition space.

– *Brian Deans* and *David Brown*, information on Trams.
– *W.A.C.Smith*, for information on Railways.
– *George Lane*, for locating rare postcards of Hyndland.
– *Gillian Mawdsley*, for communicating her longstanding interest in Glasgow's West End.
– *Chris Castell*, (Paperdart), ideas on the printed word.
– *Alma Topen*, for items from Partickhill's local history.
– *Ian Henderson* and other descendents of figures involved in Hyndland's history.
– *John Christie* and *John R Hume* (Hyndland Parish Church).
– *Ken Goodwin* (Hyndland Secondary School).
– *David McCubbin* (St Bride's Episcopal Church).
– *Hugh* and *Heather O'Brien* (Hyndland Bowling Club).
– *Jim Arthur* (Alexander Arthur & Sons).
– *George Henry* (Queensborough Motors and Hyndland Honda).
– *Many residents of my neighbouring tenements*; *Janette Stewart* and others working on reminiscences; *Sandra Cameron* for Scottish Records Office research.
– *Many other Hyndland residents* for various contributions.

Errors and omissions are entirely my own: corrections or contributions are welcome, preferably in writing.

Finally I must thank my husband, Kelvin Tyler, whose computer expertise and general support have smoothed the way on innumerable occasions throughout my work on Hyndland's local history.

Listed Buildings in Hyndland

"Listed Buildings" are afforded special protection under Town and Country Planning legislation. Buildings are listed by the Secretary of State for Scotland following surveys carried out by Historic Scotland. Reviews of listings are regularly undertaken. Neither the exteriors nor the interiors of listed buildings may be altered without prior Listed Building Consent, obtainable from the local planning authority.

Category A	of national or international importance	Hyndland Parish Church
Category B	of regional or local significance	St Bride's Episcopal Church
		The Royal Bank of Scotland
		Airlie Building, Hyndland School
		Kingsborough Gardens
Category C	of more modest architectural or historic interest	(none in Hyndland)

Hyndland lies within the Glasgow West Conservation Area and all buildings therein are covered by Conservation Area legislation. Glasgow City Council is responsible for enforcing Listed Building and Conservation Area controls.

West End Websites

Hyndland Local History	http://www.hyndl.demon.co.uk/
West End Festival	http://www.westendfest.demon.co.uk/
Glasgow West Conservation Trust	http://users.colloquium.co.uk/~GLASGOWWEST/home.htm
Friends of Glasgow West	http://users.colloquium.co.uk/~GLASGOWWEST/FGW/FGW.HTM

Views of the West End from Glasgow University Tower, 1905

WNW view from the University Tower, showing part of Hyndland

Courtesy of T & R Annan & Sons Ltd, Glasgow

Leiper's Dowanhill Church, an important West End landmark, stands at the left with its splendid Gothic spire. Just behind, a tenement is under construction in North Gardner Street. The broad roof of Hyndland Church is at the right of the photograph, with only the chimney of Kelvinside Electric Power Station visible behind. Above the curved front of Crown Circus is the long dark line of red sandstone tenements on the west side of Hyndland Road, and to the right of these, a single tenement is highlighted in the sun. Standing on the east side of Hyndland Road, looking down Queensborough Gardens, it appears to be under construction, with its unslated roof catching the light. Running along in front are the curved roofs and dormer windows of Kingsborough Gardens.

In the immediate foreground, a row of six tenements with some trees in front stands in University Avenue (now University Place), and to the left is part of the Western Infirmary. The tenements lining both sides of Byres Road run from left to right. Dowanhill Park occupies the large open plot of ground between Dowanhill Church and the square-roofed Dowanhill School.

NW view from University Tower

(Note: Hyndland is just off this picture to the left.)

In this superb photograph, one of a series of eight taken on 19th July 1905, Messrs. Annan captured a view of some of Glasgow's finest residential districts in their heyday: Hillhead, Dowanhill and Kelvinside. Interestingly, despite the density of Glasgow's population at the time, the city was still closely surrounded by open fields.

By the time the Annans returned to photograph the scene in the 1930s, the open fields between Kelvinside and the Maryhill gasometers were built over by Mactaggart & Mickel's Kelvindale estate. (The only remaining open space being the Kelvinside Academy playing fields at Balgray — the light area at the left of the view.)

In the Victorian West End itself, little has changed aside from the demolition of the west side of Lilybank Gardens (lower centre) for the planned expansion of the University campus. In the middle of the view is the curved terrace of Athole Gardens; just above it is the large slate roof of St. Luke's Greek Orthodox Cathedral in Dundonald Road. Standing prominently to the north (right) of St. Luke's is the large classical villa in Great Western Road known as "Redlands", built around 1871 for the Mirrlees family.

In the distance, immediately above Redlands, stands a building with a tall chimney, which housed the Kelvinside Brick Works (near the top of Cleveden Road). Bricks with a trademark imprint of "Kelvinside" were often used for internal walls in West End houses and are now occasionally discovered during alteration works.

Fortunately, the West End escaped the worst excesses of Glasgow's postwar redevelopment and has enjoyed status as an Outstanding Conservation Area for a quarter century. Yet these fine tenements, terraces and villas are now 100 to 150 years old and thus require special care and much investment if they are to survive well into the 21st century.

Gordon R. Urquhart
Glasgow West Conservation Trust